FIRST DRAFT

*EXPLORING THE HISTORY
OF WESTERN COLORADO
AND EASTERN UTAH*

ROBERT SILBERNAGEL

LITHIC PRESS
FRUITA, COLORADO

Cover photo: Little Dolores 2 – A group of Grand Junction people
on an outing at the 2V Ranch in the 1890s. The La Sal Mountains
in Utah are barely visible in the background. *Ela Family Collection.*

ISBN 978-1946-583-291

LITHIC PRESS
fine books for an old planet

www.lithicpress.com

Dedicated to the many people who have offered suggestions regarding possible history columns and who have provided assistance in tracking down critical information. It is also dedicated to my wife Judy, for her proofreading skill and her unflagging support of my history endeavors.

CONTENTS

PUBLISHERS NOTE

———

The key of the future is written now when it is seen
–Philip Lamantia in his poem, *Oraibi*

Upon seeing the paintings on the cave walls at Lascaux the artist Picasso said, "we have learned nothing new." History demands that we see ourselves in larger time frames. It's humbling to be aware of human history and to see the rise of civilization as a most remarkable and fragile occurrence in the history of the universe—along with stellar evolution and fresh peaches! As we navigate the conundrums of day-to-day life, it's helpful to know that others have been here before and struggled with similar conflicts inherent to being human in civil society. Lithic Press began with an urge to enhance the conversation of our community. Conversation is the glue that holds civilization intact. Through conscious effort we use our brains to work toward acceptable compromise. It's not easy.

The world is indeed in a time of turmoil as we begin to comprehend the ramifications of what is taking place before our eyes: rapidly changing climate, accelerated mass migration, economic disparity. Bombarded as we are with news, we continually hear of places where conversation has broken down, where war, chaos, instability and suffering become the norm. In the face of these difficulties there are often calls for a return to a *more peaceful time*, a fanciful notion that, at the very least, does not help us move forward with our problems. The stories in this collection show that every time of human history has its own particular dilemmas. We can never return but can learn from the past to try to improve our future, hence, this is a forward-looking book.

I've long enjoyed Robert Silbernagel's articles in the *Grand Junction Daily Sentinel* and it's an honor to make of this collection a more durable artifact. Enjoy these stories and imagine the thousands of years that Native Americans lived in this area, and the more recent canal builders, farmers, politicians, and all the remarkable and utterly common citizens who long ago struggled through doubts and uncertainties and somehow carried on to survive. After a lifetime studying natural history, the biologist, Edward O. Wilson summed up the meaning of life as, the epic of the species, the stories we tell. With this in mind, think of the words you use, your daily actions, the story you are living, the history you are writing everyday, and think about what you want to leave behind.

Danny Rosen
Lithic Press

INTRODUCTION

————

Welcome. This book is a collection of my "First Draft" history columns that have appeared in *The Daily Sentinel* newspaper of Grand Junction, Colorado, since 2013. They demonstrate my fascination with what occurred in this region in years past. I have long been obsessed with reading, researching and writing about history. I would probably engage in these activities even if no one else was interested. However, the fact that so many readers have told me how much they enjoy reading my history stories – in my books and my *Daily Sentinel* columns – makes my obsession even more enjoyable. That continuing interest and support from readers convinced me to publish another book of my *Sentinel* columns. In doing so, I hope to create a permanent record of my columns and to reach people who haven't read them in the *Sentinel*.

I wanted to have the book published locally, if possible. So, I contacted Danny Rosen, owner of Lithic Press in Fruita, Colorado, to ask if he would be interested. To my great delight, he was, and this book is the result of our partnership.

My columns in the *Sentinel* are published under the title, "First Draft," a reference to the famous quote often attributed to former *Washington Post* Publisher Philip Graham: "Newspapers produce the first rough draft of history." No matter who coined the phrase, it's an appropriate title because most of my *Sentinel* columns rely in part on early newspaper articles to recount historical stories. Readers will see that in the list of "Sources" that appear at the end of each column published here. Often, in addition to those early newspaper articles from *The Daily Sentinel* and other newspapers in Colorado and Utah, I have listed more recent sources such as books, journal articles, and personal interviews. And some columns involve subjects for which no newspaper articles were ever written.

All columns in this edition involve historic events and activities that took place on Colorado's Western Slope or in Eastern Utah, or both. For the most part, the columns herein appear as they originally appeared in *The Daily Sentinel* or at www.gjsentinel.com, with only minor editing or additions. However, several times I wrote more than one column about a particular subject. In these cases, I have combined and edited the columns into one chapter.

The columns in this book are divided into eight parts, ranging from "Agricultural Awakening" to "Outdoors Calling." If I had arranged the categories strictly in alphabetical order, Agriculture would have come first. But that's not the reason I placed the category at the beginning.

In Colorado's high country, along with other parts of the Rocky Mountains, the search for gold, silver and other minerals drew prospectors, get-rich-quick artists, gamblers and grifters. Eventually, full-time settlers arrived, along with businessmen, teachers and preachers, and they established communities. However, along the lower reaches of what was known as the Grand River (now the Colorado) and in the Uncompahgre and Gunnison river valleys, it was agriculture, not mining, that promised livelihoods – perhaps even riches – to those willing to work the land. The same was true of the broad valleys of Eastern Utah. Without the people who were willing to engage in strenuous agricultural labor, these areas would not have developed as they did. Those early farmers and ranchers hacked sagebrush from large swaths of ground to create pastures and hay meadows, and they hauled water in buckets to irrigate the earliest fruit orchards and vineyards. They created roads and promoted railroad service. They needed banks, stores, hotels and government edifices, all of which became the foundations of the towns and cities that developed in this region.

Those hardy settlers built their farms and ranches on lands once occupied by Native Americans – most recently, by Utes. Before the Utes were other ancient people. So the second category in this book is called, "The People Who Came Before." It contains columns about the Utes and earlier inhabitants of the region. It also reiterates the fact that these Native people didn't simply disappear once white settlers claimed their homelands. They are actively involved in Colorado and Utah today.

Also, before most settlers arrived, while Utes still controlled much of the territory, others began arriving in the region. There were traders, explorers, military expeditions and members of the Church of Jesus Christ of Latter-day Saints – known as Mormons. Some of these early arrivals sought only profits from beaver furs and other pelts. Some sought to escape religious persecution. Others, often with government backing, examined the region for possible railroad routes or began the process of mapping it. Still others helped protect the settlers who arrived here, as well as the Natives. Columns about them are in the third section, called "Traders, Surveyors, Saints and Soldiers."

Once the settlers came, they created a variety of communities with different philosophical and political structures. Often, colorful people joined in the creation of these communities. They are reflected in the two sections called "Communities" and "Characters."

Those same hardy settlers also demanded law enforcement and a criminal justice system to apprehend and punish people who had no respect for private property or even human life – police officers, judges and courts that would keep the chaos at bay. So, the next part in the book is called "Crime and Justice."

To get from place to place, whether within a town, or from town to town, or from the Western Slope and Eastern Utah to other locations, developing trails into roads and embracing new technologies for travel became critical.

Part VII, called "Travel Tendencies," is about those efforts.

Finally, even the hard-working farmers and ranchers, as well as their urban neighbors, quickly developed a love for recreation in this rugged landscape. Much of that recreation took place on public lands. The final section in this book reflects those pursuits, still prevalent today. It is called "Outdoors Calling."

My quest to learn more about history has led me to research and write several books on regional history. One of those books, *Historic Adventures on the Colorado Plateau*, is also based on my *Daily Sentinel* columns. This book contains columns that weren't included in that 2018 book.

None of these columns or categories is meant to be a deep dive into regional history. Rather, they offer snapshots of the area's history, glimpses into certain times in specific locations. But taken together, those snapshots, like pieces of a puzzle, provide a broader picture of Western Colorado and Eastern Utah history. Even so, nothing says readers must start at the front and read to the end. Each column is a stand-alone piece, and readers should feel free to peruse them in whatever order strikes their fancy.

I hope you enjoy *First Draft* and that you find the columns within interesting and entertaining, as I did while preparing them. Readers can learn more about my other books and columns at my website, *www.bobsilbernagel.com*.

PART ONE: AGRICULTURAL AWAKENING

Smudge Pots – A post card from the early 20th century depicts smudge pots being used to protect fruit crop from freezing. *Bowman Family Collection.*

MRS. J.P. HARLOW WITH HER FRUIT EXHIBIT FROM HARLOW FRUIT

CHAPTER 1:
FIRST FRUITS – J.P. AND KATE HARLOW

———

By the time they arrived in Grand Junction, Colorado, in 1881, John Petal (J.P.) and Kate Harlow had traveled widely and J.P. had held a variety of jobs. In Memphis, Tennessee, J.P. had been a lawyer and a teacher. Later, he worked as a miner in South America, a mining superintendent and a railroad clerk in Utah. Kate Sherman, born in Upstate New York, lived for many years in Chicago, where she was reported to be a friend of Senator Stephen Douglas and newspaper publisher Isaac Cook. She then lived in Omaha, Nebraska, for a time, before marrying Harlow and settling first in Gunnison, Colorado, then in Grand Junction and on their ranch near Palisade, Colorado.

J. P. Harlow was the first justice of the peace in Grand Junction beginning in 1882. In 1883, he was appointed a deputy United States marshal in the community. However, Harlow's most significant endeavor in the region was as a fruit farmer. He and Kate established one of the first fruit farms in the area, on Rapid Creek, a few miles east of where the town of Palisade eventually developed. They also constructed one of the first irrigation ditches in the region. They convinced many others that raising fruit was not only possible, but profitable in the Grand Valley.

Harlow was born about 1830 in Canada, although the exact location is not known. He next appeared in the official record in Geneva, New York, where he married his first wife, Elizabeth Augusta, in 1854. The couple then moved to Memphis, Tennessee, with Elizabeth's parents. A son, William, was born there in 1855.

When Elizabeth and her parents returned to New York, Harlow did not accompany them. Instead, he headed west, smitten with gold fever. He first went to Salt Lake City, Utah, then he headed to South America in search of mineral wealth, before returning to Utah. In 1870, he was listed as a railroad clerk in Ogden, Utah, and by 1874 he was a mining superintendent. He married Kate after Elizabeth had died in New York. The couple moved to Gunnison in 1878 and opened a restaurant in 1880.

However, J.P. was always searching for greener pastures. When the Grand

———

Image on left: Kate Harlow in Grand Junction, selling fruit from the Harlow Ranch on Rapid Creek. *Image courtesy of the Museums of Western Colorado.*

Valley opened to settlers after the Utes were removed in the fall of 1881, he and his wife moved to Grand Junction, a tiny community in the heart of the Grand Valley. Kate again operated a small restaurant. The Harlows also homesteaded 160 acres on Rapid Creek.

By the spring of 1882, the Harlows had planted peach trees and perhaps a few apple trees, as well as vegetables on the Rapid Creek property, convinced the region was prime country for growing fruit. The first trees died, however. Undaunted, they planted a second crop, using bone meal as fertilizer. And this time they provided irrigation water from Rapid Creek, the first ditch built in the area.

Despite J.P.'s judicial jobs in Grand Junction and the restaurant Kate operated in town, the Harlows moved permanently to the Rapid Creek farm, called the Harlow Ranch, in 1884. By then a sandstone house had been completed on the property. Harlow divided his time between Grand Junction and Rapid Creek.

Kate played a critical role in Harlow Ranch. An 1893 newspaper profile described Kate as "a woman with all the force of character usually found in manhood, and one who has through ardent toil built for herself a home" on the ranch land she developed with J.P., which was called "a tract of land as finely cultivated" as any in Colorado.

By 1886, the Harlows' ranch had more than 2,000 peach trees, 200 apple trees and a variety of other fruit trees. Their orchard was thriving.

"The year 1887 proved to be even more successful for the Harlows than the previous one," wrote William Kirk Bunte in a 1994 article about Rapid Creek. "The judge's efforts paid off with an excellent fruit crop which supplied his own table and also won first place for the best plate of peaches at the Mesa County Fair in October. Moreover, Harlow had sent peaches to the Denver Exhibition in September and had won a blue ribbon there, as well."

About this time, the Harlow Ranch became an important stop for travelers. "Bunkhouses and barns were constructed to provide a waystation for freight haulers on their way to and from Grand Junction to Mesa and Collbran," Bunte wrote. The Harlow Ranch was situated along one of the earliest roads in Mesa County. It had excellent water for horses, and was a convenient stopping point for those headed to Mesa or Collbran, Colorado, on the flanks of Grand Mesa.

In early 1884, J.P. and another man started a coal mine near Rapid Creek. He also purchased residential lots to develop in Grand Junction. In December 1886, Harlow attempted to expand his coal mine, with Grand Junction founder George Crawford as his partner.

Meanwhile, Kate raised a flock of turkeys, which she took to Grand Junction to sell, along with fruit and vegetables for extra cash.

But J.P. Harlow still was restive. In January 1889, Harlow and another man opened a real estate office in Grand Junction. In May, he was among a group of local citizens who visited recently discovered gold fields in Utah. With Crawford, he opened the Brunswick Hotel in Grand Junction. Beginning in May 1890, the Harlows also operated a post office on their ranch, which was officially called, Harlow, Colorado. It closed in April 1891.

In March 1891, while in Grand Junction, J.P. fell ill. He died of pneumonia on March 12, 1891. His body was taken to the ranch on Rapid Creek, where he was buried and a large stone monument was erected.

Kate soon leased the land on Rapid Creek, visited it frequently and routinely brought fresh fruit to friends in Grand Junction. She was among the best-known women in Grand Junction, according to *The Daily Sentinel*, and owned property in the town. She visited the Chicago World's Fair in 1893. At the Harlow Ranch, she had constructed "a fine set of buildings under her own direction, and they are commodious and elegant, of white sandstone."

Kate's time in Mesa County ended abruptly and mysteriously. *The Sentinel* said she and a man named James Gribben disappeared during the annual Peach Day celebration in the valley in 1895. But Gribben returned to Mesa County a short time later, with a power of attorney for all of Kate's assets, allegedly signed over by her. "It required but little time for Gribben to make away with the best portion of the money the old lady [Kate was 64 in 1895] had left on deposit and to dispose of ... the fine farm, which was known throughout the state as Harlow Ranch," according to a December, 1896 edition of the *Sentinel*.

Gribben apparently abandoned Kate after fleecing her. In 1896, she married a man name Otto Seigle in Missoula, Montana. It is not known when and where she died.

The Rapid Creek property changed hands several times, but it was still known as the Harlow Ranch and still producing fruit, into the 1920s.

Sources: "A History of Rapid Creek," by William Kirk Bunte, Journal of the Western Slope, Volume 9, Number 4; Author interview with Winnie Mading in 2013; Historic newspaper articles at www.newspapers.com.

CHAPTER 2:
W.P. ELA – PIONEER RANCHER, COMMUNITY
LEADER, ADVENTURER

The ranch on Western Colorado's Little Dolores River, owned by the Palisade Land and Cattle Co., was a scenic location. One early visitor described it as "a rancher's paradise and a cowboy's delight." But there was nothing easy about operating a cattle ranch in an isolated part of Mesa County during the 1880s and 1890s. Consider just one year, 1895:

That year, ranch owner Wendell Phillips Ela, better known as "W.P.," dealt with the death of one of his cowboys – unfortunately nicknamed "Calamity Bill" – who was killed after being thrown from his horse while chasing a steer. Another day in 1895, a young man was killed while driving a load of timber down the main wagon road from Piñon Mesa, Glade Park, and the Little Dolores. The wagon apparently upended on the rocky ledges and pinned the man beneath it. The road was called Jacob's Ladder because it was so rough, and W.P. Ela helped pioneer it. Today's smoother version is known as Little Park Road.

Not all the dangers were in the remote country, however. Also in 1895, four of Ela's cows jumped off the Fifth Street Bridge and drowned when a herd of about 250 was being driven to stockyards in Grand Junction, Colorado. Ela himself could have been injured or killed that year when a train on which he was traveling while shipping cattle derailed east of Pueblo, Colorado. The engineer and brakeman were killed, and several others were injured.

When he wasn't ranching in 1895, W.P. Ela also served as the Grand Junction school board president. Also that year, he helped assess the possibility of building a railroad up Plateau Canyon. Two years later, Ela was elected mayor of Grand Junction and became president of the Mesa County Bank. He and his wife Lucy had a home in the city, in addition to their ranch on the Little Dolores. Ela also was a longtime member of the Grand Junction Camera Club and the local Academy of Science, and president of the new Library Board.

Despite his busy schedule, W.P. actively managed the ranch until the turn of the century. He took cattle shipments east and rounded up what *The Daily Sentinel* called "wild and wooly" horses at the ranch. He led a *Grand Junction News* correspondent on a tour of the ranch in 1897.

"The Ela ranch is as fine a natural site for stock raising as can be found anywhere in America," the unnamed correspondent raved. He was less enthusiastic about galloping down a steep mountain slope after Ela, who was an accom-

W.P. Ela on his horse, Bourbon. *Image courtesy of the Museums of Western Colorado.*

plished horseman. The correspondent said he was "practically helpless" on the back of an Ela ranch bronco, "but by hanging close to the saddle we managed to get along without any serious injury."

W.P. Ela was born in 1849 in New Hampshire to Jacob H. and Abigail Ela. His father was a printer, state legislator and congressman before becoming Auditor for the U.S. Treasury. As a young man, W.P. Ela worked as a shipping clerk on a Hudson River steamship. But, his life changed in 1883, after his brother, Charles S. Ela, invested in the Colorado ranch. Charles died in Denver in October 1883, just as the ranch was being organized, and W.P. was drafted as a temporary ranch manager. His sojourn in the West lasted 46 years, until his death in 1929. W.P. Ela acted first as agent for the Palisade Land and Cattle Co., later as owner of what was also known as the 2V Ranch because of its brand. In addition to the ranch winter headquarters on the Little Dolores, the 2V had summer range on Piñon Mesa and along West Creek in Unaweep Canyon.

Getting to and from the ranch in the early days was difficult. If one didn't travel via Jacob's Ladder, there was a route called the Billy Goat Trail, which, as its name suggests, was no easy jaunt. "The Billy Goat Trail went up No Thoroughfare Canyon [in what's now Colorado National Monument] and went through the Rim ... right where the tunnel goes through now," said W.P. Ela's grandson, the late Bill Ela. Horses and cattle frequently slipped and stumbled on the steep rocky trail. And W.P. had a close call when a horse he was riding, appropriately called "Looney," refused to turn on one of the switchbacks of the Billy Goat Trail and instead jumped off a 15-foot ledge. Horse and rider were uninjured.

At some point, a man named John Gordon widened the Billy Goat Trail and operated a toll road through No Throroughfare Cañon. But, according to Lucy Feril Ela, mother of Bill Ela and daughter-in-law of W.P. Ela, the cattle ranchers on Piñon Mesa didn't think much of Gordon's "terrible road" and the high fees he charged. In order to avoid Gordon's toll road, W.P. "helped survey out the present road to Little Park," Lucy recalled. Even so, Lucy said her mother-in-law, who was also named Lucy, once had to utilize Gordon's Toll Road to get from the ranch to Grand Junction quickly when she was suffering from a toothache. Although Gordon's road was faster than Jacob's Ladder, it still took her nine hours to reach Grand Junction.

Both Lucy Feril Ela and Bill Ela said that in the early years of the ranch operation, Ute Indians were frequent visitors to the 2V Ranch. On one occasion, W.P. told Lucy that "the Indians camped for thirty days right up behind them and that they would come every day but they didn't give them any trouble."

In May 1901, the *Sentinel* reported that Ela "sold his fine cattle ranch on the Little Dolores to Messrs. Frank Sleeper and Sam Pollock." But he and his family continued to visit the ranch for many years. And W.P. continued to be involved with livestock.

In November 1903, Ela and several other Grand Junction men traveled east and purchased a rail carload of Kentucky Thoroughbreds. Ela bought 46 brood mares and two of the top stallions in Kentucky, the *Sentinel* reported. Later, he often led parades in Grand Junction, astride his Thoroughbred named Bourbon.

He and Lucy were active members of Grand Junction's social elite, when they weren't traveling – to Denver, to Salt Lake City, to California, to the Chicago World's Fair, or to W.P.'s native New Hampshire. In 1901, W.P. and Lucy took an extended trip across Europe, which included bicycling part of the way.

In 1905, Ela joined a group of seven other men in an unsuccessful attempt to run a steamboat from Green River, Utah, down the Green River to its confluence with the Grand (now Colorado) River, then up the Grand to Moab, Utah. The trip was abandoned two miles up the Grand. "The dream that this boat was to go up to Moab has vanished," Ela wrote in a journal he kept of the trip. "No steamer could make those rapids."

But, if the steamer didn't reach its goal, it gave Ela and his friends the opportunity to visit ancient Native ruins along the Green River, and for Ela to photograph them.

"It's a beautiful morning and I can see the sun shining on those cliff dwellings up the river," Ela wrote. Even so, he grumbled about the unreliable steamboat engines that delayed their progress. "We sit here in the deep shadow of the canyon while the engines kick, puff, dance a two-step and then quit," he wrote on one occasion. "Gasoline engines may be all right when they get going but they are not the thing to depend on a hundred miles from civilization."

Despite early antipathy toward gas-powered engines, W.P. Ela was credited with being the first man to drive a Ford automobile from Denver, across the Continental Divide to Grand Junction. He later joined the 1912 Midland Trail automobile expedition from Grand Junction to Salt Lake City, promoting a transcontinental auto highway route.

Ela's wife Lucy died in 1925, and W.P. died of pneumonia in 1929 at St. Mary's Hospital. But his considerable legacy lives on. Much of the former 2V Ranch is now protected in a permanent conservation easement. Ela Family Orchards continue to operate near Hotchkiss, Colorado under the direction of Steve Ela, one of W.P.'s great-grandsons. The former Ela family home at 1006 Main Street in Grand Junction is now the headquarters of Colorado West Land Trust, which oversees the conservation easements for both the old 2V ranch and the Ela family orchard.

Sources: Author interviews with Shirley Ela and Tom Ela; Oral history interviews with Lucy Feril Ela and William (Bill) Ela, conducted for the Museums of Western Colorado; historic editions of The Daily Sentinel at www.newspapers.com; "Log of the City of Moab," by W.P. Ela, courtesy of Tom Ela.

CHAPTER 3:
BREEZES, FREEZES AND RESILIENCY
HIGHLIGHTED PEACH INDUSTRY

Early in the 20th century, a Denver newspaper wrote that a single peach tree near Palisade, Colorado, was worth more than an entire acre of wheat, and that the Book Cliffs north of the town were worth at least $2 million "in cold cash" for the radiant heat they provide to peach growers. Exactly how *The Denver Post* arrived at those figures in 1909 is not clear. However, it is clear the newspaper was engaging in a bit of home-state boosterism when it described the irrigated orchard land around Palisade as "the most productive agricultural land in the United States."

Even so, the article's basic premise – that the Book Cliffs from Mount Garfield east to the mouth of De Beque Canyon provide important radiant heat to the orchards in the area – is correct. However, that's only part of the story, said Horst Caspari, head of the viticulture program for Colorado State University's Western Colorado Research Center. Equally important to the radiant heat from the cliffs are the breezes that flow out of De Beque Canyon into the valley like water flowing in the Colorado River, Caspari said. The breezes, which help stave off freezing temperatures, disperse as the valley opens to the west.

The combination of radiant heat and the valuable breezes can mean a difference of a few critical degrees in temperature on a frosty night when peach trees and grapevines are blooming, he said. The temperature difference between Palisade and the Lower Valley – from the town of Fruita, Colorado, west to the Utah border – can be as much as 20 degrees.

But that doesn't mean the breezes and cliffs always provide adequate protection. Many hard freezes have severely damaged or nearly destroyed peaches in the east end of the Grand Valley. The blizzard that blew in the weekend of May 1, 1915, and dropped temperatures well below freezing, caught many growers by surprise. It also led to gloomy predictions about the future of the fruit business.

"Is the Fruit Industry in the Grand Valley doomed to Failure?" a Grand Junction *Daily Sentinel* headline asked in late May 1915. Another Colorado newspaper that month declared that, "The frost of last week ... has completely ruined approximately 90 percent of the orchards" in the Grand Valley. Throughout May of that year, there were conflicting reports of how widespread the damage was and which areas suffered the worst. There were also stories of some fruit growers attempting to hastily sell their orchards.

However, the same *Sentinel* article that raised questions about the future of the industry, urged diversity for crops and tenacity for growers. "The trouble with most people is that they give up too easily," the paper said.

As it turned out, 1915 wasn't the worst year for fruit growers during the early decades of the 20th century. April freezes in 1908 and 1911 caused more severe losses. Nevertheless, the 1915 freeze not only provoked significant hand-wringing in the region, it also prompted a variety of ideas to encourage more diversity in crop production, as well as government efforts to assist those fruit growers who suffered most seriously.

As for the 1909 claim that a single peach tree was worth more than an acre of wheat, that's not true today. But it's not far off the mark. Using numbers found on a Kansas wheat tracking site, and those from a 2013 Western Colorado Research Center document called "The Cost of Growing Peaches in Western Colorado," it would require six peach trees in Palisade to provide the same gross revenue as an average acre of Kansas wheat field. The comparison is based on 2018 wheat prices, but 2013 peach prices. Peach prices have increased since then.

The 1909 article described the irrigated lands around Palisade as "the famous home of the Elberta peach, and the Jonathan apple, and the Royal Duke cherry and the Clifton cantaloupe, and sundry other gustatory aristocrats." It added, "Eleven years ago, this stretch of orchards and prosperous homes lay desert."

That wasn't completely accurate. The first irrigation ditches serving the orchard lands at the east end of the valley – on Rapid Creek and around Palisade – were constructed well before 1898. But the article was correct that irrigation made a huge difference. Before irrigation water, land in the Palisade area could have been purchased for $50 an acre, the 1909 article said. "Now it sells, by the acre, and half acre, and quarter acre, for from $2,500 to $4,500 an acre, and is hard to get at that."

Although those prices may sound high for Palisade's early history, there is separate corroboration for them. Sidney Jocknick, who moved to Western Colorado before Colorado became a state in 1876, published a book in 1913 called *Early Days on the Western Slope of Colorado*. In it, Jocknick touted "the beauties of Palisade, with her magnificent landscape of peach orchards, which have no rival on Earth and which sell from $1,000 to $4,000 per acre."

The town of Palisade was incorporated in 1904, five years before the laudatory article in *The Denver Post*. But there would have been little to entice people to Palisade if it weren't for irrigation water. Development of that important resource began in the 1880s on Rapid Creek and in 1890 at Palisade with work on the Mount Lincoln Ditch, which eventually became the Price

LOADED FOR MARKET, PALISADE, COLO.

Kluge Avenue Looking Southwest – Horses pull a wagonload of peaches down Kluge Avenue in Palisade. *Palisade Historical Society.*

Ditch, operated by the Palisade Irrigation District. The Mesa County Irrigation District was formed in early 1906 and assumed ownership and operation of the Stub Ditch. It wasn't until 1915 that the Government Highline Canal began delivering more dependable irrigation water to the Price Ditch and Stub Ditch and to more acres from Palisade to the west, beyond Fruita.

Even so, times were tough for the first peach growers. Many dropped out because of freeze losses or market conditions. But the persistent ones remained, people like a former newspaper editor named J.S. Oliver, "who didn't know any better than to hang on," according to the 1909 *Denver Post* article. "When the ditch caved in and no water came down for the trees, he hauled water in barrels from the river and saved his young trees. Now he is worth a quarter of a million dollars and spends his winters in Europe."

More trouble came in the 1920s, when an infestation of coddling moths forced the destruction of all apple trees in the East Valley orchards. Brutal freezes in the winter of 1962-1963 and again in 1989 destroyed not just the annual fruit crops, but many of the peach trees themselves. Additionally, an abundance of peaches grown nationwide sometimes caused peach prices to fall dramatically and made peach raising barely profitable.

With each setback, some growers turned to other crops or sold their orchards. But many more remained in the business, rebuilding orchards and starting new ones. Modern techniques were employed to fight the freezes and insects – smudge pots, windmills, new pesticides and organic treatments. As a result, in the first half of the 21st century, the fruit industry – especially peach growing – remains a critical component of the Western Slope's agricultural economy.

Sources: "A Cliff that absorbs sunshine and turns it into gold," The Denver Post, March, 1909, courtesy of Wanda Beebe.; "The Cost of Growing Peaches in Western Colorado," by Ron Sharp, Horst Caspari and Amaya Atucha, Western Colorado Research Center; "Peaches and Politics in Palisade, Colorado," by Paul H. Bardell, Jr.; author interview with Horst Caspari; www.kswheat.com/growers/10-year-average-kansas-wheat-production; Historic newspapers at www.newspapers.com and www.coloradohistoricnewspapers.org.

CHAPTER 4:
GARMESA FARMS BRIEFLY SOUGHT
TO MAKE THE DESERT BLOOM

Robert Lazear was a callow but ambitious Midwesterner when he arrived in Western Colorado in 1913, determined to engage in scientific farming. For the next seven years, Lazear managed Garmesa Farms, 12 miles north of Fruita, Colorado, on 16 Road, near the Garfield-Mesa County line, hence the name.

Before he arrived at Garmesa, Lazear "never had been on a farm and didn't know a field of clover from a sugar beet patch," according to a *Technical World* magazine profile of Lazear in 1915. The article by T.W. Ross added that Lazear, then 24 years old, "is a young Chicago chap who grew tired of club life in the city."

During his time in Mesa County, Lazear drew statewide praise for his enlightened agricultural practices, particularly in raising purebred Holstein dairy cows and Duroc hogs. His animals and their offspring regularly won prizes at agricultural shows throughout Colorado. He and his wife, Helen, were popular in Mesa County, supporting a variety of community activities.

But Lazear couldn't beat the mud and sand that ran off the Book Cliffs and dumped silt in a reservoir he built to provide irrigation water for the farm. By 1920, Lazear had had enough. He abandoned Garmesa, sold off its equipment and livestock, and moved to Wyoming.

A native of Illinois, Lazear graduated from the University of Michigan in 1912 with an engineering degree. But he soon set his sights on the West. He "took a six months course in the Colorado Agricultural College," Ross wrote, "then went into Western Colorado, where he took up a one-hundred-sixty-acre desert claim."

Online records at the Mesa County Clerk and Recorder's office show that Robert Lazear filed a patent for land on May 13, 1914. Why he chose such isolated property is unknown. Others had tried to farm in the area, with little success.

Lazear had financial backing from his wealthy father, George Lazear, a well-known businessman in Evanston, Illinois, and others. The senior Lazear reportedly "headed a syndicate that took up three thousand acres surrounding the youth's claim." One member of that syndicate was Henry Crowell, a friend of George Lazear and the founder of the Quaker Oats Co. Records at the Clerk's office show that in August, 1914, Henry Crowell purchased two parcels of property near Garmesa from existing landowners.

In the spring of 1913, *The Daily Sentinel* newspaper in Grand Junction, Colorado, reported, "The Garmesa company begins the cultivation of fine soil on Ruby Lee Mesa northeast of Fruita this week." That's the first printed reference to Garmesa I've found, although articles in 1912 told of construction of a reservoir at Ruby Lee Mesa. Lazear built the reservoir, just west of 16 Road, as the main water supply for Garmesa Farms. He later raised the dam on the 21-acre reservoir to provide twice as much water.

Ross wrote that enlarging the reservoir "settled" the farm's irrigation problem, but that clearly wasn't the case. Three years later, Lazear and his men were still struggling to clear silt from the reservoir.

Lazear was a busy man during his years at Garmesa. He returned to Illinois in the fall of 1913 to marry Helen Gerould. Meanwhile, he had a stately house constructed at Garmesa for his planned family. His brother, Edward, moved to Garmesa to join him, and another large house was built for Edward.

Twenty bachelor employees slept in a bunkhouse at the farm, while other employees and families had their own houses. One early employee, Charlie Wilson, became the foreman. He and his wife became caretakers of the property after Lazear left.

Garmesa Ruins – Concrete foundations were all that remained from Garmesa Farms, north of Fruita, when this photo was taken in the 1960s. Now, there is even less to show where the farm once operated. *Image courtesy of the Museums of Western Colorado.*

In 1914, Lazear worked to make the wagon road from Fruita to Garmesa suitable for automobiles. He also acquired an automobile and a large truck, which the *Sentinel* said would be used "in transporting visitors to and from the Garmesa Orchard." Later, Lazear urged the Mesa County commissioners to construct a proposed new road from Fruita to Rangely, Colorado, up 16 Road and over the Book Cliffs. It was eventually built three miles to the west on 13 Road.

Lazear consulted experts on farming practices. On their advice, he used dynamite to blast holes for his fruit trees "which loosened the soil for several feet around."

He constructed his own weather station to predict freezes, although his apple and pear orchards never produced fruit.

Drinking water for the Lazears and their employees, as well as the farm's livestock, came from the reservoir, but he installed a distilling system to make it fit for human consumption.

He sought advice on the best seed varieties to plant for oats, sugar beets and alfalfa. He compared growth from different seeds and determined which were most drought tolerant.

He maintained detailed data for his livestock, tracking how much food they ate, their weights and daily milk production for his cows. A modern dairy barn was constructed, with the latest in manure handling and milking equipment.

By 1916 he was advertising Holstein cows for sale and touting their milk production in comparison to other dairy breeds. In 1917, he conducted a series of on-site tours for farmers from Plateau Valley of Colorado and from Delta and Montrose counties, so they could see a modern dairy and hog operation. That same year, at age 26, Lazear was named president of the newly formed Intermountain Livestock Organization. He and Helen helped found an organization for school children interested in livestock. Garmesa was also a popular spot for Grand Valley residents on weekend outings.

Then, with little public warning, Lazear gave up on Garmesa. In March 1920, an advertisement appeared in the *Sentinel* saying, "Garmesa Farms will hold a gigantic sale of stock and farm machinery at its ranch 12 miles north of Fruita, Wednesday March 31st."

After the sale, Lazear moved to Wyoming. He, his father and brother became officers in Henry Crowell's newly purchased Wyoming Herford Ranch, and Robert became ranch manager. "There were a lot of men out there who had lots of opinions and traditions. But they couldn't think of new ways to do things." Crowell said later. But Robert Lazear "was eager to try new things."

Lazear's association with the Hereford ranch proved far more successful than his time at Garmesa. He was manager there for 37 years. When he died in 1957, publications around the country extolled his reputation as ranch manager and breeder of some of the top purebred Herefords in the country. Some articles noted that he had lived in Western Colorado briefly. Few mentioned Garmesa.

In the meantime, Garmesa had been "abandoned to the coyotes and the ravages of time," according to a Montrose, Colorado, newspaper. The buildings at the farm had been sold and hauled away. The Lazear house was purchased by Lloyd Olsen and moved to Fruita. There was a decades-long flurry of oil and gas drilling near Garmesa, with limited success. These days, a number of small home plots dot the desert near where Garmesa once operated.

Sources: "Farm Experiment in the Desert," by T.W. Ross, in Technical World Magazine, March 1915, at www.hathitrust.org; Historic newspapers at www.newspapers.com and www.coloradohistoricnewspapers.org; "Cereal Tycoon: Henry Parsons Crowell, Founder of the Quaker Oats Company," by Joe Musser; additional information from Ike Rakiecki, librarian at Mesa County Libraries.

CHAPTER 5:
SUGAR BEATS TOOK ROOT
IN WESTERN COLORADO

When the sugar beet harvest began in Mesa County, Colorado, in September 1907, it was expected to be a good one. The weather had been reasonable that summer, even though a late frost hurt the orchards. More and more farmers had planted beets. The sugar beet factory in Grand Junction had overcome initial obstacles and was working smoothly.

By October, the *Palisade Tribune* in Palisade, Colorado, could proclaim: "The great plant is running along in splendid shape. There has not been a serious hitch in its operation since the season opened." *The Tribune* added, "The quality of beets is first class, and the fact that this is a superb beet raising country has been most emphatically proven."

The Daily Sentinel in Grand Junction, Colorado, provided data to back up those statements. By October 19, 1907, the sugar plant had produced 40,000 tons of sugar from beets, more than double the 16,000 tons produced through the same period the prior year. It was manufacturing an estimated 700 tons of sugar "each and every day."

Less than a decade old in 1907, the sugar beet industry was already important locally. An estimated 6,000 acres of beets were planted that year in Mesa County and nearby counties. It didn't yet rival the fruit industry, with an estimated 20,000 acres of trees in 1907, but it was growing rapidly. And it wasn't just Grand Junction. Throughout much of the 20th century, sugar beet production was "the most important agricultural activity in the state," according to the *Colorado Encyclopedia*. More than 20 sugar refining factories were built in Colorado between 1899 and 1920.

Grand Junction's was the first – a three-story brick building, the interior of which was larger than a football field. A portion of the building still stands across from the Las Colonias Amphitheater at the south end of 12th Street in Grand Junction. The plant began production in November 1899 as the Colorado Sugar Manufacturing Co. In 1902 it was sold to a Wyoming firm, the Western Sugar and Land Co. In 1916 it was sold again to the Holly Sugar Co., which continued to operate it full-time until 1929, then intermittently until 1933.

But sugar beet production didn't end in Western Colorado when the Grand Junction plant closed. Holly Sugar continued to operate a beet plant in Delta until 1977. An estimated 10,000 acres of beets were cultivated in Mesa, Delta

Sugarbeet workers – Harvesting sugarbeets was hard work and required plenty of laborers, including children, as this photo from the late 19th century or early 20th century in the Grand Valley demonstrates. *Image courtesy of the Museums of Western Colorado.*

and Montrose counties in the 1970s. Now, the only sugar beet production in Colorado is on the Front Range, and it's a fraction of what it once was. But for nearly 80 years, sugar beets were among the most important cash crops in this region – one that farmers could count on for an annual paycheck.

Sugar beets were often referred to as "white gold." Many early investors in the industry were mining magnates or people who had made money in the mining industry, men looking to diversify their financial interests. Denver entrepreneur Charles Boettcher, founder of the Boettcher Foundation, who made his initial fortune selling mining hardware in Leadville, was on the board of directors of the group that opened the Grand Junction sugar factory. So was John F. Campion, the owner of several Leadville mines and the man credited with being "the father of the sugar beet industry in Colorado." There was no local man on the board, although Colorado Springs businessman James Renwick McKinnie had been an investor in the Grand Junction Town Co. And Charles N. Cox of Grand Junction is credited with traveling to Denver to get Campion, Boettcher and others interested in sugar beets in the Grand Valley.

However, the fledgling industry faced a critical problem. Growing sugar beets in 1907 required intensive labor. Workers had to bend and pull, shovel and lift, even crawl on their hands and knees. There was not a large enough labor force to handle all the work. In addition to the harvest, thinning and other procedures demanded large numbers of laborers. Women and children were perceived as most efficient in the thinning process, and children were an important part of the workforce. Although some Native American children from Grand Junction's Teller Indian School were employed early on, there still weren't enough workers. So, first the Colorado Sugar Manufacturing Co., and later Western Sugar, sought to attract immigrants.

Families of prospective beet growers were offered low-rent land and the possibility of buying it for $50 an acre, free water for five years and free tents for their first dwellings. Campion sent a letter to leaders of the sugar beet industry in Germany, seeking help in getting immigrants.

However, the first sugar-beet immigrants were German-Russians from Missouri, Kansas, Nebraska and Utah. German-Russians were people of German ancestry who had emigrated to Russia at the invitation of Catherine the Great in the 18th century. When political and economic conditions changed in the mid-19th century, many emigrated to the United States and Canada, especially to the Great Plains states. Later, some came to Colorado. However, within a few years of arriving in Colorado, many of the ethnic Germans had purchased their own plots of land or had become involved in other businesses. Again, more laborers were needed for the sugar beets.

World War I worsened the labor shortage, although political and economic unrest in Mexico led many people from that country to move north. Along with Hispanics from New Mexico and Colorado's San Luis Valley, a significant number of Mexicans made their way to Western Colorado to work with sugar beets. Some were employed as migrant laborers, moving to other locales when work in one community was completed, but quite a few chose to remain in the Grand Valley. Holly Sugar wanted to encourage them to stay. In the 1920s the company built two "longhouses" to house laborers west of the beet factory near the Colorado River. Over the years, individual houses were built nearby and a neighborhood of primarily Hispanic families developed that became known as La Colonia. Today's Las Colonias Park is named in honor of the neighborhood.

Even as mechanized farm equipment began to assume much of the work in the sugar beet plantings, individual workers were still necessary for many of the tasks. Hispanic laborers remained an important part of the industry until its demise.

That came without warning in early 1977 – after many farmers had already acquired seed and prepared land for the coming season – when Holly announced it was closing its Delta sugar plant. A variety of economic factors resulted in that decision, including increased competition from foreign sugar producers and a need to upgrade the Delta plant. As a result, 70 years after the booming growth of 1907, the sugar beet industry ended in Western Colorado.

Sources: "The Colorado Sugar Manufacturing Company: Grand Junction Plant," by William J. May Jr., Colorado Magazine, Winter 1978; Historic Colorado newspapers at www. coloradohistoricnewspapers.org and www.newspapers.com; "The Sugar Beet Industry," Colorado Encyclopedia, www.coloradoencyclopedia.org/article/sugar-beet-industry; 1907 Colorado Agriculture Report; "The History of Las Colonias Park," by Jonathan Car and Claire Kempa, Colorado Mesa University and the City of Grand Junction Parks and Recreation Department.

CHAPTER 6:
1909 WATER WAR ERUPTED IN THE EAST
END OF GRAND VALLEY

Whiskey is for drinking, as the old dictum says, but water was definitely for fighting over in the Grand Valley of Western Colorado in the summer of 1909. Ditch riders were deputized, court injunctions were issued and defiant irrigators were arrested and fined. A special train carried hundreds of angry water users from Palisade and Clifton, Colorado, to the Mesa County Courthouse in Grand Junction, Colorado, in late July 1909. There the water users awaited a judge's decision for the Palisade Irrigation District, which operated the Price Ditch.

Irrigators in the east end wanted their head gates left alone by ditch riders so they could use as much water as they believed they needed. But if that were allowed to occur, irrigators in the west end of the district near Clifton would have been without sufficient water for their orchards and crops.

Eventually, Palisade Irrigation District joined with its neighbor, Mesa County Irrigation District, in 1910 and 1911 to build a new diversion dam to make water delivery more dependable. In less than a decade, that new system would be replaced by yet another dam and distribution system – one that still operates today.

Palisade Irrigation District holds some of the oldest water rights on the Colorado River, dating from 1890, when a man named Frank Burger filed for private water rights for what was then called the Mount Lincoln Ditch. Later, the company operated two canals. The Mount Lincoln Ditch system went through several ownership changes until 1904. Then irrigators in the area formed Palisade Irrigation District and purchased all the land and what was known as Canal No. 1 from the company. That became known as the Price Ditch.

Two years later, another group formed the Mesa County Irrigation District and purchased the water and land associated with Canal No. 2, which is now called the Stub Ditch. The two districts had separate small dams and ongoing difficulties with their water supplies.

The problems in the Price Ditch in 1909 stemmed from recurring high water in the Colorado River, which was then called the Grand River. Excess water washed out the riverbed where the Price Ditch diversion began, making it impossible for Palisade Irrigation District meet all its water demands simultaneously. As a result, the district's board of directors and superintendent set up

Pal Irrigate – Beginning of the Price Ditch, where it takes off from the Government Highline Canal, as seen in 1920. The 1909 fight over Palisade Irrigation District water was largely settled when the Highline began supplying water to the Price Ditch. *Bureau of Reclamation publication.*

four sub-districts within the district.

Next, they instructed ditch riders to begin rationing water, making it available to each sub-district every few days. That meant closing head gates in the east end for several days at a time so that irrigators in the west end – as far west as today's 29 Road – would also have water. But that didn't sit well with orchard growers in the east area.

"Growers in a Mass Meeting Protest: Orchardists Under Price Ditch Claim Water is not Equally Divided," read a July 17, 1909, headline in *The Daily Sentinel* newspaper of Grand Junction. "New Ditch Rider Asked For." The accompanying article said orchard owners demanded "that all head gates at the upper end of the valley be opened and that every grower under the big canal be awarded his full complement of water each day." The same article said "the desired changes will probably be made at once." But that wasn't the case.

By July 22, the irrigation district had obtained a temporary injunction against some 50 east-end irrigators. *The Sentinel* said the defendants had "defied the board, the superintendent, the ditch riders, refused to permit ditch riders … to close the head gates near their ranches, but persisted in taking water … as often as they wanted it and in whatever quantities they wanted." Consequently, no water flowed to orchards in the west end of the district, and if that situation wasn't remedied quickly, the west-end orchards "will be ruined or irreparably damaged," the paper said.

On July 24, the newspaper reported that Dr. J.H. Divine, "one of the wealthiest and best known fruit growers of the Palisade end of the valley," was arrested by Mesa County Sheriff Charles Schrader on contempt of court after he reportedly violated the injunction. Divine told the newspaper he and other growers had indeed refused to allow a ditch rider to close their head gates on the day the injunction was issued. But, he said, that was before they were served with notice of the injunction.

On the morning of July 27, the *Sentinel* said, "a special train left Palisade … carrying about 200 fruit growers and other citizens" to Grand Junction. Another 100 people arrived by automobile "and vehicles of various kinds." They were awaiting a decision from a county judge on whether the temporary injunction would be made permanent. However, about 10:30 that morning, the judge told the crowd that the case had been dismissed and the injunction lifted. Palisade Irrigation District officials apparently believed they didn't have enough evidence to secure a permanent injunction. "This leaves the Palisade Irrigation District just where it was before the temporary injunction was secured," the *Sentinel* added. "For this reason, many of the growers today were heard to express dissatisfaction over the dismissal of the case."

Meanwhile, the water fight continued. On August 10, the *Sentinel* reported that J.E. Griffith and Guy Tilden, "two Palisade fruit growers, have been arrested on the charge of unlawfully interfering with the waters of the Palisade Irrigation District." A third man, August Heggbloom, was arrested the next day on a similar charge. Two weeks later, all three men were found guilty of the charges, and were fined $10 apiece, plus court costs.

The water war of 1909 appeared to evaporate soon afterward. By October, 1909, engineer Charles Vail had developed plans for construction of a single diversion dam across the Colorado River to serve both the Palisade and Mesa County irrigation districts. In December, voters in Palisade Irrigation District approved bonds totaling $88,000 to pay for their share of the work, and construction of the new dam began in January 1910. But a severe winter delayed work on the project and it wasn't completed until 1911. Meanwhile disputes with water users continued. In March 1910, a ditch rider reported that 12 new head gates had been constructed on the main canal, but only three of them had been approved by the board.

By the following year, even as the new dam and diversion system were being completed, both the Palisade and Mesa County irrigation districts were negotiating with the U.S. Reclamation Bureau to participate in the planned Government Highline Canal. They were hoping for more dependable water supplies through the government project. The two districts would remain separate water entities, but they would become a part of the new irrigation system that helped transform much of the Grand Valley beginning in 1915.

Sources: Historic editions of The Daily Sentinel through www.newspapers.com; "Chronicles of Palisade/Mesa County Irrigation District History," courtesy of Palisade Irrigation District; Resolutions and correspondence of the Palisade Irrigation District, 1909; interviews with Dan Crabtree, manager Palisade Irrigation District and Dave Voorhees, manager Mesa County Irrigation District; "The History of Irrigation in Palisade and East Orchard Mesa, Colorado," by Palisade Historical Society.

PART TWO:
THE PEOPLE WHO
CAME BEFORE

Chipeta – Ute Indian leader Chipeta, in front of blanket covered shelter in Mesa County, early 20th century. *Image courtesy of the Museums of Western Colorado.*

Teepee – Utes near a teepee in Utah's Uintah Valley, 1874., John K. Hillers, *photograph, Library of Congress.*

CHAPTER 7:
FREMONT CULTURE THRIVED IN UTAH
AND WESTERN COLORADO

———

The team of archaeologists and students who arrived in Utah from Harvard University's Peabody Museum in 1931 knew about the abundance of prehistoric ruins and images throughout the region. Even so, Nine Mile Canyon surprised them. In field notes, Donald Scott, a leader of what became known as the Claflin-Emerson Expedition, described the canyon as "almost a continuous picture gallery." Guide and photographer David Rust, a Utah native who had led archaeologists to ancient sites across much of the Colorado Plateau, wrote with amazement in his journal when he arrived in Nine Mile Canyon that there were "ruins everywhere."

Nine Mile Canyon, which is about 45 miles long, cuts through the West Tavaputs Plateau, beginning about 15 miles northeast of Price, Utah. Nine Mile Creek, which flows through the canyon, empties into the Green River. The variety of rock art throughout Nine Mile Canyon is clear evidence that ancient peoples – including those we refer to today as members of the Fremont Culture – lived in or visited the desert canyon for millennia. They built rock dwellings, shelters, granaries and what appear to be lookout buildings high on cliff tops. They grew maize, beans, and squash here. They also hunted and gathered wild grains and nuts. One of the largest rock art panels in Nine Mile Canyon is called the Hunter Panel for its hunting scenes.

In Colorado, evidence of the Fremont people has been found largely near the Utah border. Panels with Fremont rock art can be seen in the Paradox Valley just east of Utah in Montrose County; in Unaweep Canyon southwest of Grand Junction, Colorado; in Canyon Pintado near Rangely, Colorado; in Dinosaur National Monument along the Colorado-Utah border; and in Brown's Park in the northwest corner of the state.

Nine Mile Canyon in Utah didn't attract white settlers until 1886, when the U.S. Army constructed a road through the canyon to link Fort Duchesne, in the Uintah Basin, with the railroad at Price. "For some twenty years [it] was probably the most heavily traveled wagon road in eastern Utah," wrote Edward A. Geary, whose grandfather drove horse-drawn freight wagons over the road. Before construction of the Army road, some ranchers likely grazed cattle in the canyon intermittently, and residents of communities such as Price, Wellington and Helper, Utah, probably explored in the area. But the first hardy settlers didn't appear in the canyon until after the road was built.

The earliest documented references to a Nine Mile Canyon in Northeastern Utah are from journals written in 1871 by men who were part of John Wesley Powell's second expedition down the Green and Colorado rivers. Powell included the same canyon name in his 1875 book about the expedition. However, as author Jerry Spangler noted, the canyon called Nine Mile in the Powell documents is 42 miles downstream on the Green River from the canyon today known as Nine Mile. What Powell and his men called Nine Mile is today known as Rock Creek.

Perhaps Nine Mile Canyon received its name because the surveyor for Powell's 1871 expedition used a nine-mile triangulation process, as one theory has it. Another story claims that the name wasn't related to distance at all. Instead, it involved early settlers named Miles, who had seven children, so a total of Nine Miles in the family. In the 21st century, the name's origin remains a mystery.

It was clearly known as Nine Mile Canyon in July 1931, when the Claflin-Emerson Expedition arrived and spent about two weeks exploring the canyon on horseback. The Harvard crew documented some of the most important ancient Native sites in the canyon, while ignoring or missing other prominent sites.

The Harvard men weren't the first scientists to explore Nine Mile Canyon. At least since the 1890s, amateur and professional archaeologists had been visiting the remote canyon. Like many explorers of the time, most were interested in collecting artifacts and selling them to museums or to private collectors rather than carefully excavating and documenting what they found. By the late 1920s and early 1930s, better organized and documented explorations of Nine Mile and other Fremont sites had begun.

The first solid definition of what we now call the Fremont Culture was offered by another Harvard man named Noel Morss. He visited Nine Mile Canyon and other parts of Utah in 1928 and 1929. Morss published several papers about the mostly agrarian Fremont society that thrived in Western Utah and parts of Nevada, Idaho, Arizona, Wyoming, and Colorado from approximately AD 1 to 1500 AD. But it was Morss's 1931 treatise, "Ancient Culture of the Fremont River in Utah," that firmly established the Fremont people as a distinct culture, similar to the Ancestral Puebloan people of the Four Corners, but with significant differences in the way they lived, their homes and the artifacts left behind.

The Fremont Culture wasn't monolithic. It is now believed that the people who shared this culture – who lived in this region for at least 1,500 years – may have included groups who spoke different languages and had different tribal customs. Even so, they had much in common. People of the Fremont Cul-

Hunter Panel – This famous petroglyph rock art panel from Nine Mile Canyon in Utah is believed to depict and ancient hunting scene. *Robert Silbernagel photo.*

ture utilized isolated stone storage facilities that modern archaeologists believe served as granaries. The Fremonts developed a distinctive basketry style called "one-rod-and-bundle." They had moccasins made from the hocks of deer or mountain sheep. They wore hair bobs, headdresses and necklaces, and developed a gray pottery style using coiled clay. But rock art is the most visible relic of the Fremont Culture today – petroglyphs and pictographs that include trapezoidal human figures, many with unique head adornments.

For decades after the Claflin-Emerson Expedition and into the 21st century, archaeological exploration of Nine Mile Canyon occurred sporadically. Planned gas drilling near the canyon accelerated research early in this century.

The most recent research shows that Fremont people inhabited the canyon for longer than what was previously believed. They may have arrived in Nine Mile Canyon as early as AD 250 and intermittently inhabited Nine Mile until as late as 1200 AD. Other locations in Utah and Colorado show even earlier occupation by people of the Fremont Culture, and they remained in other locales later than had previously been reported. One site near Rangely, Colorado, shows evidence of Fremont occupation until almost 1600 AD.

Several rock art styles not associated with the Fremont Culture have also been found in Nine Mile Canyon. But Fremont rock art is dominant. The prevalence of such art in Nine Mile Canyon "exceeds anything reported elsewhere in the state of Utah and maybe even the United States," Spangler wrote. Moreover, much of the canyon has yet to be investigated by archaeologists.

Sources: "Nine Mile Canyon: The Archaeological History of an American Treasure," by Jerry D. Spangler; "The Crimson Cowboys: The Remarkable Odyssey of the 1931 Claflin-Emerson Expedition," by Jerry D. Spangler and James A. Aton; "Nine Mile: Eastern Utah's Forgotten Road," by Edward A. Geary, in Utah Quarterly magazine, winter 1981, reprinted in fall, 2017; "9 Mile Canyon" at www. blm.gov; "Fremont Culture," by Michael Metcalf, at www.coloradoencyclopedia.org/article/fremont-culture.

CHAPTER 8:
DOMESTIC CHORES MARKED
UTES' USE OF UNCOMPAHGRE SITE

About 1870, a small group of Ute Indians gathered on the east side of the Uncompahgre Plateau in Western Colorado to engage in domestic chores. The group – probably an extended family band – spent weeks or even months at what is now called the McMillen Trade Goods Site. The Utes who stopped there refurbished their ammunition. They created beadwork and metal decorations for their clothing and their horse bridles. They cut metal from flattened tin cans to make cone-shaped decorations known as tinklers. They used metal tools such as a triangular metal file, a crude tweezers and a folding pocketknife.

"It's one of those sites where you feel like the people who were here walked away from it yesterday," said Curtis Martin of Palisade, Colorado, the principal investigator for The Wickiup Project, which conducted a recent archaeological assessment of the McMillen Site.

For example, Martin noted, there was a nearly straight line of small glass beads tracking across a good portion of the seven-acre site. "Someone walked across the site or rode a horse with a broken bead string," he explained. Elsewhere, the glass beads and the metal items were deposited in concentrated clusters, evidence of where the Utes of 150 years ago spent time working on them.

Martin led the assessment of the McMillen Site in August 2021 and completed a report a year later for the History Colorado-State Historical Fund. Colorado Preservation Inc., a Denver-based nonprofit group that works to preserve historical sites, acted as the administrative organization for the project.

An earlier study of the McMillen site showed the 1870s Utes weren't the first Natives to visit. There is evidence of brief Native occupations dating to the Archaic period, perhaps 1,000 years ago. Those visitors worked to flake arrowheads and spear points from stone. There were no metal materials or tools for them, no glass beads or horses.

More recent visitors were prehistoric Utes who lived in this region prior to contact with Europeans or soon after the Spanish arrived in New Mexico. Pieces of Ute brownware pots found on the site are evidence of this.

Anthropologists believe the Utes were part of a group of Uto-Aztecean speakers who migrated north from Mexico before 1,000 A.D. They first appeared as a distinct culture in the southern part of the Great Basin – southern

Nevada and Eastern California – approximately 1,000 years ago. They expanded east across the Colorado Plateau and into the Central and Southern Rocky Mountains. Their language is related to those spoken by Paiutes, Bannock, Shoshone, Gosiutes, Comanche, and tribes in Southern California and Mexico.

The Utes tell a different story, however. As the website for the Southern Ute Tribe says: "The Utes do not have a migration story. The Utes have always lived here in the mountains." Some Utes say the Fremont people were their ancestors. Although archaeologists cannot prove such a link, some of the Fremont people lived similar lifestyles to the Utes in the same geographical areas.

By the 1870s, the Utes were clearly the dominant people of Eastern Utah and Western Colorado, traveling across both desert and mountain landscapes. The McMillen site that Martin and his crew investigated is west of Montrose, Colorado, on U.S. Bureau of Land Management property on the edge of the Uncompahgre Plateau.

The first study of the site was conducted by University of Colorado archaeologist William G. Buckles in 1961, while he was still a graduate student. He wrote about it and other Ute sites in his 1971 doctoral dissertation. In 1961,

Tinkler – A piece of decorative metal believed to have been made by Utes from a metal can. Found at the McMillen Trade Goods Site. *Curtis Martin photo.*

Buckles dug artifacts at the site and took them to a laboratory to be examined.

Sixty years later, when the site was re-examined by Martin and a team that included Holly "Sonny" Shelton as crew chief, and two anthropology students from Colorado Mesa University, as well as several other volunteers, they adhered to a strict "non-collection" strategy. All artifacts they found were photographed and described at the site, then returned to the exact location and depth where they had been found.

The items Buckles collected 60 years earlier are now archived at the BLM's Canyons of the Ancients Museum and Visitor Center in Dolores, Colorado. Martin was able to examine them in conjunction with his assessment of the McMillen Site. He also worked closely with the BLM and officials with the Ute Tribe in Fort Duchesne, Utah, and the Southern Ute Tribe in Ignacio, Colorado, in determining how to explore the site while protecting culturally sensitive items. His team used a metal detector to find many of the metal trade goods, while the glass beads were discovered on the surface, or in small mounds near the surface.

However, they found no remnants of wooden structures such as wickiups, storage sheds or brush fences – structures that Martin has studied for nearly 20 years as lead investigator first with the Colorado Wickiup Project and now with what's simply called the Wickiup Project. "The uniqueness of this site is that it's covered with trade goods, but there is no evidence of wood structures," Martin said. "So, as we examined the site, we tried to find evidence of where there might have been wickiups or other wooden features."

Because no wooden structures were found, the team could not use tree rings to date the site. However, Martin's team had two other sources to indicate when the Utes visited the site.

First, were the glass beads. Throughout his career, Martin has learned that glass beads were larger during the earlier decades of European/American trade with Natives. As the trade continued, the Natives sought smaller beads for decorations, and the glass-making companies in Europe complied. Based on the tiny beads found on the McMillen site, Martin is convinced the site was occupied between 1860 and 1880.

Evidence from ammunition at the site was even more specific. Photos of shell casings and spent bullets or musket balls were sent to Douglas Scott, a retired National Park Service archaeologist and an expert in 19th century weaponry in the American West. "Doug said nothing we found was from before 1868, and none of it was made later than 1880," Martin reported. Since that fit closely with the dates established based on beads, Martin is confident Utes occupied the site sometime from the late 1860s through the 1870s.

Weaponry artifacts provided evidence that the Utes had at least one muzzle-loading rifle, based on a .50 caliber ball and percussion cap that were found.

Additionally, the Utes must have had several Henry or Winchester repeating rifles, based on spent cartridges. A tiny ball, likely fired from a small-caliber rifle or a shotgun, was also found.

Ammunition from a big-bore Spencer rifle showed the resourcefulness of these Utes, who apparently had no Spencers of their own. The team found several empty Spencer cartridges that had not been fired. The Utes at the McMillen site "pried out the lead and took the gunpowder" from the Spencer ammo to make ammunition for their own weapons, Martin said.

Also discovered were buttons made from shells, ball buttons, and tubular glass beads. Altogether, the team found 221 different artifacts at the McMillen Site. "The findings were above and beyond what we expected," Martin said. They demonstrate that Utes in the latter half of the 19th century not only had up-to-date trade goods, but they were adept in using or modifying them to suit their needs.

Martin and his team have recommended the site for the *National Register of Historic Places.* Even though it was not threatened by human activity when Martin's report was written, that designation would help protect it if threats arise. Martin has also recommended periodic monitoring of the site to ensure it is not being damaged, as well as some test excavations that could help determine where there were wickiups, campfire hearths or other important features.

Sources: Author interview with Curtis Martin; Introduction to "The Archaeological Assessment of the McMillen Trade Goods Site in Montrose County, Colorado," by Curtis Martin. "Ute Creation Story," Southern Ute Indian Tribe. www.southernute-nsn.gov/history/ute-creation-story; "A History of the Northern Ute People, by Fred A. Conetah; "Ute History and the Ute Mountain Ute Tribe," by James M. Potter. www.coloradoencyclopedia.org; "The Ute Indians of Utah, Colorado, and New Mexico," by Virginia McConnell Simmons.

CHAPTER 9:
CHIPETA REMAINED IMPORTANT
UTE LEADER THROUGHOUT HER LIFE

As the wife of the Ute leader Ouray, the woman called Chipeta was well known to white settlers in Western Colorado in the 1870s. After her husband died in 1880, Chipeta remained an important leader for her band of Utes for the next 44 years, and she became even better known to whites than she had been while Ouray was alive. But there was also a lot of misinformation about Chipeta.

For instance, a 1921 photo of Edith Abbott Green of Grand Junction, Colorado, shows a square-faced woman with penetrating eyes and dark hair adorned with a sparkling headband. On the back of the photo, a typewritten caption says Green is "Wearing a Beaded Headband from Chipeta, Queen of the Ute Indians." But the caption adds a note that suggests Chipeta's economic situation was bleak. Chief Ouray's famous widow, who had once enjoyed material wealth, traded the headband to Green "for a loaf of homemade bread," it says.

Chipeta was often called "The Queen of the Utes" by whites, first as a derogatory remark, but later as a sign of respect. However, it is clear that by the 1920s, when she resided on a ranch at Bitter Creek, near Dragon, Utah, Chipeta was not living like royalty.

As early as August, 1911, *The Daily Sentinel* in Grand Junction reported that friends of Chipeta had started to raise money for the Ute woman, who, the paper reported, was "almost destitute." It added, "The old woman, whose husband was the best friend the early white settlers had among the Indians, is nearing the century mark." Actually, in 1911, Chipeta was only 68 years old, having been born in 1843. She was far from "nearing the century mark."

But inaccurate stories about Chipeta were not unusual. Here are some others:

Chipeta was born a Ute princess. She was probably born a Kiowa, but was adopted by a Ute family after she was discovered as a toddler, wandering among the bodies of her Kiowa relatives who had been massacred by unknown attackers.

Chipeta and Ouray had a son together. Chipeta likely never gave birth to any children. But she helped raise Ouray's children as well as her own adopted siblings. Throughout her life, she adopted or cared for several children. Ouray's son, known as Pahlone or Paron, was born to his first wife, Black Mare. After she disappeared, and Ouray married Chipeta in 1859, Chipeta treated the youngster as her own son. But Paron was kidnapped by Sioux warriors while the Utes were hunting on the Front Range in 1863. He was traded to Arapaho Indians and became known as Ute Hanna. He grew up in Wyoming and never reunited with his Ute family.

In 1879, Chipeta *"rode four days and nights to rescue the white women and children held as hostages by the hostile Utes"* following the killings of Nathan Meeker and his employees at the White River Indian Agency. This persistent story apparently was started by a Denver newspaper editor in the 1880s. But Chipeta's own words disprove it.

"I was at my house when they [the hostages] came there" after they were released by the White River Utes, she told the Congressional Committee on Indian Affairs in 1880. "General Adams came with them." Charles Adams was the man who went to the Ute camp and negotiated the release of the women and children. Ouray's sister, Susan or She-to-wich, who was sometimes confused with Chipeta by whites, had protected the hostages during their captivity.

It's also debatable just how destitute Chipeta was in her later years. There is evidence that her economic situation was partly of her own choosing. In 1916, during conversations with Albert H. Kneale, superintendent of the Ute reservation school in Utah, Chipeta dismissed the notion that she needed more compensation from the U.S. government. "I am as well provided as are other members of my tribe. I desire nothing," she told Kneale. "I am not better than they and what is good enough for them is good enough for me."

Even so, Chipeta had lost much since her life with Ouray. Before the 1879 killings of Meeker and his employees led to the removal of most Colorado Ute Indians to Utah, Chipeta and Ouray lived in a large adobe house near the Uncompahgre River south of present-day Montrose, Colorado. Household furnishings included a piano, fine china and many items they had received as gifts from white friends. They had a farm and many head of cattle, sheep and prized horses.

But Ouray died of kidney disease in August 1880, as the treaty was being completed that would require the removal of the Uncompahgre and White River Utes from Colorado. When that forced exodus occurred in 1881, Chipeta joined her fellow Uncompahgre Utes on the long march to the new reservation in Utah, even though she was initially told she could continue to live in the house she had shared with Ouray. Chipeta had barely left that house when federal authorities decided to sell off her household belongings without consulting her.

Chipeta was promised a new home in Utah as good as the one she had abandoned in Colorado. Instead, she received a house that, according to one

Chipeta – Chipeta and her husband Chief Ouray, wearing a shirt she beaded. *Colorado Women's Hall of Fame.*

Indian agent, was "tiny, poorly built and unfurnished." There was a rough table and wooden boxes served as chairs, but little else. Chipeta spent most of her time in traditional Ute lodgings – a teepee or wickiup on her land at Bitter Creek. She still had plenty of cattle and sheep. And she likely joined other Bitter Creek Utes on annual trips to Mack, Colorado, to ship some of her livestock to market on railroad cars.

The Sentinel reported that Chipeta visited Grand Junction "on average about once a year." On one such trip, in 1923, she was treated for cataracts at St. Mary's Hospital.

Even though Chipeta was comfortable living frugally, she and other Utes had plenty of reason to be frustrated. For one thing, a promised government-built irrigation ditch was never constructed, leaving much of their land unusable. Additionally, white settlers were allowed to purchase reservation lands from the Utes, often at ridiculously low prices, under a law known as the General Allotment Act. Also, Utes on the reservation often complained of inadequate food and of treaty commitments that weren't being upheld.

Chipeta demonstrated her leadership by frequently contacting government officials and pushing for better treatment of the Utes. In one letter to the Commissioner of Indian Affairs she reminded him of the government pledge to build irrigation ditches. Since that had yet to occur, the Utes had built their own ditches in some areas. But white farmers had taken the water by building their own irrigation ditches upstream of the Utes. "We have lands, it is true, but without water, these lands are of no value," Chipeta wrote.

Still, Chipeta remained friendly to whites. In the 20th century, Colorado inhabitants sought to honor her in a variety of ways. She joined President William Howard Taft in his car during the 1909 ceremonies opening the Gunnison Tunnel as part of the Uncompahgre Valley Irrigation Project in Montrose. She also visited the communities of Ouray, Colorado Springs, Durango, and Grand Junction on various occasions, and was treated as a celebrity, enjoying automobile rides and motion pictures.

Chipeta was also known for her fine beadwork and for making traditional Ute apparel. She gave items such as finely beaded moccasins and purses to white friends. So, Edith Abbott Green's headband may have been a simple gift from Chipeta, not the act of an impoverished woman desperate for a loaf of bread.

Chipeta died on Aug. 16, 1924, at her home on Bitter Creek, and was buried nearby. People in Colorado soon pushed to rebury her next to her husband Ouray, but that reunion never occurred. Chipeta's remains were moved to Montrose and were buried on the property where the Ute Indian Museum now sits. Ouray's body was eventually moved to the Southern Ute Reservation in Ignacio, Colorado.

Sources: Historic editions of The Daily Sentinel at www.newspapers.com; "Chipeta, Queen of the Utes," by Cynthia S. Becker and P. David Smith; "Chipeta, Queen of the Utes, and Her Equally Illustrious Husband, Noted Chief Ouray," by Albert R. Regan and Wallace Stark, Utah Historical Quarterly, July 1933.

CHAPTER 10:
BLUFF, UTAH, BATTLE WAS ONE OF LAST
INDIAN CONFRONTATIONS

—————

A dispute over a campfire card game, the subsequent murder of one of the participants and the search for the accused murderer near Bluff, Utah, sparked one of the last armed Indian conflicts in the United States in February of 1915. However, the antipathy between the Utes and white ranchers in Four Corners region had simmered for years. It had far more to do with issues related to use of the public range and traditional Ute hunting grounds than a conflict over cards.

The card game and shooting of sheepherder Juan Chacon occurred in March, 1914. His body was found in Southwestern Colorado a few days after he left the card game, and Utes friendly to the whites accused a 27-year-old Ute man named Tse-ne-gat – known to whites as Everett Hatch – of having murdered Chacon, then leaving his body in an arroyo.

Although he initially seemed ready to turn himself in, Tse-ne-gat and his father Polk decided they would do better hiding out in the rugged country between Bluff and Grayson, Utah (now known as Blanding). After repeated demands from Bluff and Grayson residents, and the urging of Utah's governor, U.S. Marshal Aquila Nebeker of Salt Lake City finally formed a posse nearly a year later, in February of 1915, to track down and arrest Tse-ne-gat and Polk. The posse was made up of nearly 75 men from Southeastern Utah and Southwestern Colorado.

They tried to surround Tse-ne-gat and Polk, along with Polk's band of about 30 Utes, on February 21 near Bluff. A small group of Paiutes led by another man named Posey was nearby and also became involved. A gunfight ensued. One member of the posse, a man from Dolores, Colorado, and at least two Indians were killed. Nebeker unsuccessfully pursued the Indians for several weeks.

When Tse-ne-gat and others finally surrendered, it was to an aging Army general who met the fugitives, assisted only by one aide and a Navajo interpreter.

The fight near Bluff wasn't the last armed battle between whites and Indians. But it was close. And issues linked to it — the refusal of some Utes and Paiutes to live on reservations and continued friction with ranchers over livestock grazing — would linger for years.

Utes have lived in Southeastern Utah for centuries, but after Congress

McElmo Bluff – A rock formation in McElmo Canyon, Utah, in the area near where Te-se-ne-gat lived. *William Henry Jackson photo, Library of Congress.*

passed a law in 1880, they were expected to move to a new reservation in Southwestern Colorado. Posey's band of Paiutes also had deep roots in Southeastern Utah. The Paiutes and Utes refused to live on the Colorado reservation because of limited water and grass for their livestock, and because they believed the Utes in Colorado were hostile to them. Animosity between whites and Natives in Utah continued, even though some ranchers supported the Indians.

In 1903, Posey was accused of stealing a horse, but the charges against him were dropped. In 1907, Polk and Tse-ne-gat angrily confronted white ranchers attempting to force their cattle from traditional Ute grazing lands in Montezuma Canyon, east of Monticello, Utah.

Most of Montezuma Canyon is in Utah, ending at the San Juan River. But smaller canyons that feed into it stretch into Colorado. "The canyon has been home to the Anasazi, Paiutes, Utes, and Navajos, as well as Euro-Americans in the various guises of cattleman, trader, settler, and miner seeking its resources," wrote author Robert McPherson. The canyon "served as a natural thoroughfare for hunters and gatherers as well as stockmen who capitalized on the resources of river and mountain. The water that runs down the canyon encouraged small agricultural plots that depended upon both flood and pot irrigation techniques."

No one who used the canyon regularly, least of all the Utes, wanted to be pushed from it. Consequently, there were confrontations between Natives and whites.

Despite these encounters, a 1908 report prepared by the superintendent of the Fort Lewis Indian School near Durango, Colorado, said the Utes in Mont-ezuma Canyon were peaceful and prosperous and were not a threat to whites. But other reports and local officials argued that the Indians killed livestock, were a threat to whites and should be forcibly removed to Colorado.

When Tse-ne-gat — who already had a reputation as a troublemaker — was accused of the Chacon murder, whites in the region were eager to see him arrested and his band removed from Utah. Newspapers in Colorado and Utah tracked Marshal Nebeker's month-long effort to find and capture Tse-ne-gat, along with those hiding him.

"Armed Posse is After Renegade," read a headline in a Moab, Utah, news-paper in mid-February 1915. Many articles reported that an armed battle be-tween Nebeker's posse and the Utes and Paiutes with Tse-ne-gat was imminent.

The anticipated gun battle occurred on the morning of February 21, when posse members thought they had surrounded the Utes and could force them to surrender. "But the Indians heard them and immediately opened fire," ac-cording to a Salt Lake City newspaper. "Joe Atkins of Dolores, Colorado, fell at the first volley. Firing continued for some minutes and two Indians were seen to fall over dead."

Tse-ne-gat, his father, and their followers escaped farther into the moun-tains near Comb Wash, Utah. Nebeker spent a frustrating few weeks attempt-ing to track down the Indians, often in wet and snowy conditions. He agreed to stand down and disband his posse only when he was informed that Army Chief of Staff General Hugh Scott was on his way to resolve the situation.

On March 8, 1915, *The Daily Sentinel* of Grand Junction, Colorado, an-nounced Scott's arrival in Grand Junction by train. He continued by rail west to Thompson, Utah, then headed by wagon to Bluff in hopes of negotiating with the Indians. It was a risky mission, the paper declared. In fact, newspapers across Utah and in Colorado gave Scott little chance of success. Only over-whelming military force would corral the renegades, most people believed.

But Scott was sanguine. "Yes, I'm going in alone," he told one newspaper. "I'm satisfied that I can settle this trouble without the aid of soldiers. I've done it before." Scott had a record of successfully negotiating with restive Native groups, from the Philippines to the American Southwest.

His efforts to end the conflict in Southeastern Utah were at first hampered by bad weather. Finally, on March 20, 1915, at a trading post in Mexican Hat, Utah, Scott accepted the surrender of Tse-ne-gat and several others, includ-ing Polk and Posey. The general accompanied seven of them to Salt Lake City, where all but Tse-ne-gat were eventually released after they promised to move to the Colorado reservation. They did so, but soon returned to Utah.

By the time Tse-ne-gat's trial began on July 9, 1915, in federal court in Den-ver, he was a popular figure in the city, reportedly receiving red neckties, pink stockings and love notes from local women. The trial featured claims of witness intimidation and an Indian agent who angered the prosecution by supporting Tse-ne-gat. After nine days, Tse-ne-gat was acquitted. He left Denver, waving from the back of the train as crowds cheered him. He returned to the lands he loved in Utah, and he briefly served as a member of the Ute tribal police in Colorado. He and his father had other disputes with whites near Bluff and Blanding and in Montezuma Canyon. Tse-ne-gat died from tuberculosis in 1922.

Friction between the whites and Indians continued into 1923. Then the trial of two Utes accused of stealing from a sheepherder, and their escape before sentencing, prompted another posse to chase the latest offenders, who soon allied with Posey's band. There was another brief gun battle. Most of the Indians soon surrendered, and about 80 men, women and children were housed in a temporary wire-fence stockade in Blanding for several weeks, before being released. Posey refused to surrender. He was wounded in the initial battle, and died several weeks later, probably from complications from his wound.

The Last Indian Uprising had ended. The small group of Utes and Paiutes were allowed to remain in Utah on individual land allotments. Most eventually settled on White Mesa, south of Blanding, Utah, and became known as the White Mesa Utes.

Sources: Utah historic newspapers at www.digitalnewspapers.org; Colorado historic newspapers at www.coloradohistoricnewspapers.org and www.newspapers.com; "As if the Land Owned Us, an Ethnohistory of the White Mesa Utes," by Robert S. McPherson; "A History of Utah's American Indians," by Forrest S. Cuch; "Canyons, Cows, and Conflict: A Native American History of Montezuma Canyon, 1874-1933," by Robert McPherson, Utah Historical Quarterly, November 1992.

CHAPTER 11:
NATIVE FAMILIES ARE CONNECTED
THROUGH 1863 KIDNAPPING VICTIM

———

When the late Harold Ouray was a boy growing up on the Northern Arapaho's Wind River Indian Reservation in Wyoming, he was known as Harold Smith. At the time, there was an old man who frequently visited the Smith family. "His name was Jack Johnson," Harold recalled. He was a Ute Indian from Utah and Harold's relative.

When Jonas Grant Bullethead was growing up on the Ute Indian Reservation near Fort Duchesne, Utah, his great-grandmother, Clara Thompson Johnson Wopsock, recounted the Johnson family's lengthy history. It included stories about Jonas's great-great grandmother, Susan Johnson, the sister of famed Ute Chief Ouray, and how Ouray's only son, Paron, was kidnapped by Sioux in 1863, while Ouray and other Utes were hunting buffalo on the plains northeast of Denver.

Paron, also known as Pahlone and Cotoan, was traded to an Arapaho chief, who raised him as his son. As a man, Paron became known as Ute Hanna, and he served as a scout for Army General George Crook during the campaign against Sioux and Cheyenne. In that capacity, he helped bring the Sioux leader Crazy Horse to Fort Robinson in Nebraska when Crazy Horse surrendered in 1877.

Records from the 1920s show that Ute Hanna received a military pension for his service as a scout for the U.S. Army during 1877. He was known simply as "Ute" when he was in the Army, and received the longer name, Ute Hanna, in the early 1900s. He died in 1931, when he was 74 years old, according to his widow Susan Hanna.

Ute Hanna was Harold Ouray's great grandfather and Jonas Bullethead's great uncle.

Jonas Bullethead and Harold Ouray have a common ancestor: Salvatore Guerro, the father of both Ouray and Susan. He was a member of the Tabeguache band of Utes but was also part Jicarilla Apache, and he was part Spanish. He married a woman who was half Jicarilla Apache and half Ute. Guerro raised his family for a time in New Mexico before returning to Ute lands in what is now Colorado. Jack Johnson, the man who visited Harold Smith/Ouray's family when Harold was a young boy, was a grandson of Susan Johnson and a half-brother to Jonas Bullethead's maternal grandfather, Myton Johnson.

Harold Ouray had a long association with the Johnson family. When he was a small boy his family visited Ute cousins at White Rocks, in Utah, north of Fort Duchesne. Harold didn't meet Jonas Bullethead until the 21st century. "But I knew of him," he added.

Jonas and his wife, Joy, assisted me with my book, *Troubled Trails*, about the 1879 Milk Creek battle and killings at the White River Indian Agency. Susan Johnson played a key role in protecting white hostages in the aftermath of those events. As we worked on the book, Jonas told me about descendants of Ute Hanna who lived on the Wind River Reservation near Riverton, Wyoming. He later put me in touch with Harold Ouray. Harold has since died, but his sons stay in contact with Jonas and other Ute family members in Utah.

Ute Hannah – Ute Hanna, aka Paron or Cotoan, as a young adult. *Courtesy of Jonas Grant Bullethead.*

Harold Smith changed his last name because of his growing interest in his famous ancestor, Chief Ouray, preferring that name to the white-man name "Smith," which was given to Harold's grandfather when he attended the Carlisle Indian Industrial School in Pennsylvania. Harold's father was raised by his grandfather, Ute Hanna, and his grandmother, Susan Hanna, Harold said. Through his father, Alexander Smith, Harold learned about Ute Hanna's history.

The Paron-Ute Hanna story took a strange turn in 1873, a decade after his kidnapping. At the time, the U.S. government was negotiating the Brunot Agreement with the Utes in Colorado. Through the Brunot agreement, the Utes agreed to give up a large portion of the San Juan Mountains to miners and settlers. To garner Chief Ouray's support, Felix Brunot, president of the U.S. Board of Indian Commissioners, said he would try to find Paron and reunite him with his father. Brunot began corresponding with E.P. Smith, then Commissioner of Indian Affairs, urging Smith to use his staff to track down Ouray's son among the Wyoming Arapahos.

Federal authorities thought they accomplished that task, and a meeting between Ouray and a young man believed to be his long-lost son was held in

Washington, D.C., in late 1873, while Ouray and his wife, Chipeta, were there for negotiations over the Brunot agreement. A partial transcript of that meeting headed by Brunot was reprinted in *Colorado Magazine* in March, 1939. Reading the transcript, it's clear that the young man, called by the name Friday during the meeting, was not eager to rejoin the Utes. And he probably was not Ouray's son.

One of the Arapaho leaders who accompanied Friday to Washington, a man called Powder Face, said that "Friday wished him to say that he could not understand the Utes, and wished to stay with the Arapahoes [Arapahos]."

Later during the discussion, Friday asked – again through Powder Face – for Ouray to say where his son was taken. When Ouray responded that the kidnapping occurred about 30 miles north of Denver, Powder Face responded, "Friday was caught in a fight further north ... Friday is not the one." The young man they sought was still in Wyoming, he said.

Ouray agreed. "The whites have tried to have me get this boy. But he is not my boy. If he was, he would not talk that way."

Despite his disappointment, Ouray agreed to the Brunot agreement, opening lands around today's Silverton and Ouray, Colorado, to white prospectors and angering many Ute leaders by doing so. Some years later, Ouray visited the Arapaho reservation in Wyoming, and met his actual son. But Ute Hanna also said he had no desire to leave his Arapaho family, and Ouray reluctantly left his only son in Wyoming.

Felix Brunot believed he had found the correct young man long after the meeting he arranged in Washington. A biography of Brunot, published after his death in 1898, quoted Brunot as saying: "All who saw them knew they were father and son, but the boy could not believe that he was not an Arapahoe." Brunot also said the young man known as Friday died during a journey to Texas about a year after his meeting with Ouray.

That was not Ute Hanna. He lived a long life. He married a Shoshone woman named Singing Woman, who became known as Susan Hanna. They had at least eight children, but only one, Minnie Hanna Smith – Harold Smith's grandmother – lived to be an adult. Susan and Ute Hanna lived most of their lives on the Wind River Reservation near Riverton, Wyoming. Ute Hanna was buried in a cemetery south of Riverton, Wyoming. In 2007, his relatives from Wyoming and Utah provided a new headstone for his grave, recognizing Ute Hanna's service to this country. Those relatives in Wyoming and Utah continue to meet regularly to recognize their joint ancestry and share their unique history as Native American families of the West.

Sources: Author interviews with Jonas Grant Bullethead and Harold Smith/Ouray; "Efforts to Recover the Stolen Son of Chief Ouray," by Ann Woodbury Hafen, Colorado Magazine, March, 1939. U.S. Army pension records for Ute Hanna and probate records.

PART THREE:
TRADERS, SURVEYORS,
SAINTS AND SOLDIERS

CHAPTER 12:
THE 1820s, WHEN TRADERS TREKKED
TO THE ROCKY MOUNTAINS

In early 1822, William Henry Ashley – entrepreneur and politician – joined forces with bullet maker and occasional fur trader Andrew Henry to place advertisements in St. Louis, Missouri, newspapers. The ads said the pair were seeking 100 "Enterprising Young Men ... to ascend the river Missouri to its source, there to be employed for one, two or three years." The men were to gather furs, primarily beaver, for what became the Rocky Mountain Fur Co.

The Ashley ad was published less than a year after Mexico won its independence from Spain and opened its borders to American traders. In September 1821, William Becknell of Missouri became the first person to outfit a small group of traders with pack horses and mules and lead them to Santa Fe, New Mexico, to legally trade in the newly independent country. He did so again the following year, this time using wagons to haul more goods, and soon the Santa Fe Trail became the most important trade and travel route in the Southwest.

Among the enterprising young men who answered Ashley's call were individuals who became among the most famous mountain men in the West: Jim Bridger, Jedediah Smith, Tom Fitzpatrick, Antoine Leroux and Jim Beckwourth. They were later credited with developing key travel routes in the West, such as South Pass in Wyoming, which would be critical to emigrants headed to Oregon, and a pathway into the Salt Lake Valley.

Ashley's Hundred, as they came to be called, weren't the only fur traders in the Rocky Mountains in the early 1820s, nor were they the first. Other trappers and traders preceded Ashley's men on the Missouri River and its tributaries. As early as 1806, John Colter, who had been a member of the Lewis and Clark Expedition, is believed to have led a small group of trappers into the Yellowstone Valley. The next year, he led a cadre that included Manuel Lisa, a New Orleans-born Spaniard who had become an American citizen, to the Big Horn River. There, Lisa established the first trading post in the Upper Missouri Basin. Two years later, Lisa formed the Missouri Fur Co. He continued to trap and trade on the Missouri and its tributaries for more than a decade.

Meanwhile, traders like Robert Stuart from John Jacob Astor's Pacific Fur

The Trapper – "The Trapper," by Leopold Grozelier. *Yale University Art Gallery, The Mabel Brady Garavan Collection.*

Co., based on the Columbia River, and Peter Skene Ogden, also based on the Columbia but with the British Hudson's Bay Co., began to make incursions east into the Northern Rockies. And in 1822, Astor created the Western Division of his American Fur Co., headquartered in St. Louis, then began sending his own traders up the Missouri River and establishing his own trading forts along the way. That led to a decades-long feud between the Rocky Mountain Fur Co. and the American Fur Co., while smaller organizations and independent traders also jostled for business.

But William Ashley did something that revolutionized the Rocky Mountain fur trade. Taking a page from the old British NorthWest Co., which had operated around the Great Lakes and in Canada, Ashley and his men didn't just build posts along the Missouri and its tributaries and wait for Natives to bring furs to them. Leaving the well-known river routes, they took pack trains of horses and mules into the Rocky Mountains to trade with Natives and to conduct large-scale trapping efforts themselves. Soon, trappers with the American Fur Co. and other groups copied them.

The earlier traders had worked on and off for years, but their business enterprises were limited, and there was little penetration to the Interior West – to the mountains of what would become Colorado, Utah, and southwestern Wyoming. Ashley's men and the Western Division of Astor's American Fur Co. changed that. Additionally, Ashley established the first Green River Rendezvous, an event that became an annual bacchanalia and attracted hundreds of trappers, traders, and travelers, and often several thousand Native Americans.

In 1825, Ashley and his intrepid crew became the first people to make a documented boat trip down the Green River – from Wyoming to the Uintah River in northeastern Utah, using bull boats made of buffalo hide and willow frames. It was not an easy trip. There were many rapids, and frequently they had to halt to repair their crude, 10-foot by 7-foot boats. "In the course of our passage through the several ranges of mountains, we performed sixteen portages, most of which were attended with the utmost difficulty and labor," Ashley wrote.

Meanwhile, traders along the Missouri River and its tributaries, as well as Becknell and others using the Santa Fe Trail, began seeking government help to protect them and their business operations from sometimes-hostile Native people. In 1818, Secretary of War John C. Calhoun authorized the Yellowstone Expedition, a thousand soldiers with steamboats and cannon who were to make their way up the Missouri River to the Yellowstone, demonstrating to Native groups along the way the power of the U.S. military.

But the steamboats couldn't handle the turbid waters of the Missouri. They foundered and were abandoned. Many of the men fell ill, and the expedition barely made it a third of the way on its ordered route. However, a smaller group under Colonel Stephen Long that had originally been a part of the Yellowstone Expedition set out again in 1820 on an overland scientific expedition up the Platte River to the eastern front of the Rocky Mountains in today's Colorado. They returned along the Arkansas River and roughly on the trail that became the mountain branch of the Santa Fe Trail.

The first military expedition to accompany traders on the Santa Fe Trail, attempting to protect the merchants from hostile Natives, didn't set out until 1829. Four companies of the Sixth Infantry from Jefferson Barracks near St. Louis marched to the border with New Mexico, a distance of more than 700 miles. Although the soldiers successfully defended themselves and merchants from an attack by Comanches, the military soon realized the infantry was a poor fit for the West's vast lands, especially when pitted against horse-mounted Indians. Soon, the U.S. Congress authorized creation of several units of dragoons, horse-mounted troops to patrol the West and attempt to forge treaties with Native groups.

These first military forays into the Rocky Mountains and the Southwest were the spearhead of an ongoing American military presence in the region. It grew significantly once American settlers arrived.

While soldiers were traipsing around the region, a man named Etienne Provost (pronounced pro'-vo) also joined in transforming the West. As early as 1815, Provost and others had been trapping illegally in Spanish territory on the Arkansas and Platte rivers, in part of what is now Colorado. He was among a group of trappers arrested by Spanish authorities in New Mexico and imprisoned for 48 days prior to 1820. But in 1822, shortly after Mexico won its independence, Provost was one of the first Americans to begin working out of Taos, New Mexico. That year, he is believed to have joined a party that pushed north and west into the Rocky Mountains. Two years later, he trekked across the Wasatch Mountains and descended into the Salt Lake Valley. The Provo River and the city of Provo, Utah, are named for him.

Joining Provost on the 1824 journey was Antoine Robidoux, another St. Louis native. Afterward, he and his brothers began hauling trade goods from Missouri to New Mexico on the Santa Fe Trail. Antoine soon moved to Santa Fe to establish himself in that community. He was elected to the Santa Fe City Council in 1827. The following year, he married the adopted daughter of the governor of Mexico. Also in 1828, he received an exclusive license from Mexico to trade and trap in the territories we now know as Western Colorado and Eastern Utah. In 1828, he built Fort Uncompahgre on the banks of the Gunnison River just west of present-day Delta, Colorado. It was the first permanent retail outlet in Western Colorado.

In 1832, Robidoux purchased a small trading post near the confluence of the Whiterocks and Uintah rivers in Northeastern Utah, which was called Fort

TO
Enterprising Young Men.

THE subscriber wishes to engage ONE HUN-
DRED MEN, to ascend the river Missouri
to its source, there to be employed for one, two
or three years.—For particulars, enquire of Ma-
ior Andrew Henry, near the Lead Mines, in the
County of Washington, (who will ascend with,
and command the party) or to the subscriber at
St. Louis.

Wm. H. Ashley.

February 13   ——98 tf

Ashley Ad – William Ashley's advertisement in the Missouri Gazette, February 1822. *Public Domain, Wikimedia Commons.*

Robidoux or Fort Winty, (short for Uintah). An inscription Robidoux chiseled into a rock outcropping west of the Colorado-Utah border shows the route he traveled between the two trading posts. Robidoux hauled his goods from Santa Fe or Taos north through the San Luis Valley of Colorado, over Cochetopa Pass, then to Fort Uncompahgre. From there he could ship goods to Utah and bring furs back the same way. His posts were also important stopping points for explorers and travelers. In addition to furs, they traded horses, guns and whiskey, and occasionally, Native slaves.

Back in the days when Manuel Lisa was active in the fur trade, one of his young employees was Charles Bent, who developed a passion for the fur trade and the Southwest. In 1833, with his brother, William, and a partner named Ceran St. Vrain, he established the important trading post known as Bent's Fort on the Arkansas River in Southeastern Colorado. For most of its brief history, the fort was the only permanent settlement on the Santa Fe Trail between Missouri and the Hispanic communities in New Mexico.

The Bent brothers and St. Vrain "built a vast mud castle that Mexico came to fear," wrote historian David Lavender. "For here was the spearhead of American expansion to the Southwest." According to the National Park Service, which manages the Bent's Old Fort National Historic site today, the Bent–St. Vrain trading empire, "radiated from Bent's Old Fort into what is now Texas, New Mexico, Kansas, Nebraska, Arizona, Utah, Wyoming, and Missouri. The fort solidified one of the most important and last established trading cartels in the Rocky Mountain West."

The fort was abandoned in 1849, after the fur trade had largely evaporated. It would take decades of commerce, westward emigration, military expeditions, war with Mexico and diplomatic negotiations with Great Britain for the vast region that includes Colorado and Utah to become the American West as it is known today. But it is clear that the early 1820s were a pivotal time in that development.

Sources: "Ashley, William H., 1825 Rocky Mountain Papers," at www.mtmen.org; "Across the Wide Missouri," by Bernard DeVoto; "Bent's Fort" by David Lavender; "Antoine Robidoux and Fort Uncompahgre," by Ken Reyher; "A History of the Robidoux Brothers in America," by Orral Messmore Robidoux; "Etienne Provost, Mountain Man and Utah Pioneer," by Leroy R. Hafen, Utah Historical Quarterly, Volume 36, Number 2, 1968; "Bent's Old Fort, Castle of the Plains," National Park Service, www.nps.gov/beol/index.htm.

CHAPTER 13:
LATTER DAY SAINTS AND U.S. ARMY
NARROWLY AVOIDED 1857 WAR

———

In late February 1858, Captain R.B. Marcy of the Fifth Infantry arrived at Fort Union, in eastern New Mexico, after a harrowing trip through the Colorado Rockies with a small troop of soldiers. He and his men had scrabbled on hands and knees in deep snow to make a path for their worn-out horses and mules, had been forced to eat many of their animals to avoid starvation, and had lost several pack animals as they descended from the top of the Book Cliffs to the Colorado River east of what is now Grand Junction, Colorado.

Their mission was to gather supplies for Army regiments stationed at Fort Bridger, in today's Wyoming, in preparation for what many believed would be a war between the United States and the Church of Jesus Christ of Latter-day Saints, known as the Mormons. The church was led by Brigham Young, who was also the federally appointed governor of Utah Territory.

The Mormons had arrived in the Salt Lake Valley barely a decade earlier. In fact, the religion itself was little more than three decades old. In 1823 near Palmyra, New York, a man called Joseph Smith was reportedly visited by an ancient prophet named Moroni. He directed Smith to a nearby hill, where he showed him engraved metal plates buried in the ground. The plates, Smith said, told a religious history of an ancient civilization in North America. Four years later, Moroni allowed Smith to translate the record. The Book of Mormon was written by Moroni's father, an ancient warrior and prophet named Mormon. It was first published in 1830.

Throughout the next few decades, Latter-day Saints, or Saints, recruited new converts enthusiastically in the United States and Europe. The LDS church grew swiftly, but its rapid growth and tightknit community also sparked burgeoning opposition from more traditional religious groups.

In response, Smith moved the church from New York to Ohio, then to Missouri, just across the Missouri River from the bustling trade and immigrant staging point of Independence. Finally, in 1839, the Latter-day Saints established the community of Nauvoo, Illinois, along the Mississippi River. They drained swamps, built a town with picturesque homes, farms, businesses and a temple. But, as in previous locations, the Saints' success and tendency to stick tightly together fostered anger, distrust and jealously in the local populace. As the governor of Missouri had done a few years earlier, newspapers in the area called for killing the Mormons. In 1844, Joseph Smith and his brother Hyrum were killed by an armed mob in Carthage, Illinois.

Brigham Young, who became leader of the church after Smith's death, began another relentless search for a new home for the Latter-day Saints. In early 1846, he led them into Iowa territory and created a settlement called Winter Quarters near present-day Omaha, Nebraska. From there, they prepared for their historic trek to the Salt Lake Valley. Young had reportedly learned of the Great Salt Lake and its potential for his flock from John Fremont's report of his second survey expedition across the West in 1843-44. Young and an advance party of Saints arrived in the Salt Lake Valley on June 22, 1847.

Over the next 22 years, according to an official church history, an estimated 68,000 Latter-day Saints arrived in the valley and other communities in Utah. But it wasn't just Utah. Under Young's leadership, Mormon pioneers established more than 600 communities from Southern Alberta to Mexico.

"Brigham Young was a colonizer without equal in the history of America," wrote author Wallace Stegner. "In a desert that nobody wanted and that was universally considered a fit home only for coyotes and rattlesnakes, he planted in thirty years over three hundred and fifty towns ... One hundred of those towns were colonized in the first ten years, when transportation was fearfully difficult and expensive, when the nearest source of many essential supplies was over a thousand miles away."

Moreover, members of the LDS church didn't just build towns. They established tight-knit communities where farming families lived within village limits and worked their land outside the villages. "By this means the people can retain their ecclesiastical organizations, have regular meetings of the quorums of the priesthood, and establish day and Sunday schools," Church President John B. Taylor, Young's successor, explained in 1882. The compact villages also provided protection from non-Mormon thieves and Indians, he said.

However, the rapid expansion of the LDS empire and those communities that were often unfriendly to outsiders provoked tension between the Mormons in Utah and the U.S. government. Anxiety grew among many in the U.S. government and people in territories and states around Utah. They feared that Young and other church leaders were intent on creating an independent, theocratic state in the heart of the West, although Young repeatedly denied it and expressed his loyalty to the United States. The Saints' acceptance of polygamy also frightened non-Mormons.

The situation worsened in March 1857 when William W. Drummond, a non-Mormon federal judge in Utah, resigned his post and claimed that the church and Brigham Young were responsible for murder, destruction of federal court records, harassment of federal officers, and slandering the federal government. In July, President James Buchanan, who had made opposition to

Marcy 2 – General Randolph B. Marcy circa 1860-1875. *Brady-Handy photograph collection, Library of Congress.*

Mormons a critical part of his 1856 election campaign, ordered the Army's Utah Expedition to take the field against the Mormons. In September, Brigham Young declared martial law in Utah and prohibited the U.S. Army from entering Utah Territory.

In the East, views differed on the pending Utah War. One newspaper in South Carolina opined that "The territory of Utah presents a spectacle of moral depravity and social degradation to which the annals of civilized man offer no parallel." The paper urged President Buchanan to do everything possible to rid the nation of Mormons. *The New York Daily Herald*, suggested that war with the Mormons would be disastrous economically and militarily and would make the nation look bad to the world. The paper said Young's actions were "treasonable," but predicted the church would join Indian allies to overwhelm any U.S. forces that attacked Utah.

Mormons in Utah took exception to Buchanan's decisions and comments from papers back East. The LDS newspaper in Salt Lake City, *The Deseret News*, declared in September 1857 that "The principles of our Government are good, and they will ever be observed and sustained by the inhabitants of Utah." But, it added, if a corrupt federal government persisted in attempting to enslave Utah residents, it would result in "the direst civil war upon record." The paper reiterated its concerns in a lengthy editorial on November 25, 1857, the day after Marcy and his troops departed Fort Bridger for New Mexico.

Fort Bridger, now in southwestern Wyoming, was then a part of Utah Territory. It had begun as a fur-trading post operated by mountain men Jim Bridger and Louis Vasquez. But the fur traders were kicked out and the small fort briefly became a Mormon Militia outpost. In 1857, the U.S. Army under General Albert Sidney Johnston, took control of the fort as an operational base against the Mormons if war occurred. But the retreating Mormons had burned most of the fort, and Johnston's soldiers were forced to live in tents. Normally, supplies could have come from places like Fort Leavenworth in Kansas. But Mormons had attacked and destroyed supply trains headed to Fort Bridger over that route. Consequently, Johnston decided to look to Fort Union, southeast of Santa Fe in New Mexico Territory, for his supplies.

He appointed Captain Marcy as the head of a detachment of 40 enlisted men, 25 mountain men, and assorted packers and guides. The chief guide was Jim Baker, friend of Jim Bridger and a man familiar with the Colorado mountains. About six inches of snow lay on the ground as they left Fort Bridger on November 24, 1857.

"My guides, as well as other mountain men, were of the opinion that we should not, at that early season, find over two feet of snow upon the summit of the mountains," Marcy wrote in a memoir published a decade later. The guides also said the detachment should reach Fort Massachusetts, at the southern end of the San Luis Valley in Colorado, within 25 days.

Instead, it took them twice that long, and the snow in the San Juan Mountains reached depths of five feet and more. Some of their beleaguered pack horses and mules died each day, and the soldiers ate most of them to stay alive. Baker got them lost in the San Juan Mountains as they tried to find the pass to the San Luis Valley. Were it not for the knowledge of Miguel Alona, a civilian packer with Marcy's party, they might never have made it out of the mountains.

They finally straggled in to Fort Massachusetts about January 15, 1858. Only one man died on the journey, a soldier who gorged himself at the fort when they finally had ample food.

Marcy and his troops moved on to Taos, New Mexico, and from there to Fort Union. Marcy gathered wagons that he filled with supplies for Fort Bridger, along with more than 100 soldiers. They headed out on March 20 and traveled north along the Front Range of the Rockies, then over South Pass in Wyoming and southwest to Fort Bridger. By the time Marcy and his troops arrived in mid-June, the threat of war between the United States and the Mormons had largely disappeared.

April 1858 saw the arrival in Salt Lake City of Thomas Kane, of Philadelphia, who had long been a friend of the Mormons, and Alfred Cumming of Georgia, who had been appointed to replace Young as Utah governor. Kane persuaded Young and other Mormon leaders to accept Cumming in the post.

In June, two peace commissioners appointed by President Buchanan arrived in Salt Lake City, carrying an amnesty proclamation for the Mormons. Church members would be forgiven for past offenses if they accepted Cumming's authority and allowed the Army to establish a garrison in Utah Territory. Young and other church leaders accepted the terms.

As a result, Johnston's army, Marcy included, marched peacefully through nearly deserted Salt Lake City on June 26 and the Utah War was over.

Sources: "Thirty Years of Army Life on the Border," by Randolph Barnes Marcy; "A Winter Rescue March Across the Rockies," by LeRoy R. Hafen, in The Colorado Magazine, January, 1927; "Mormon Country," by Wallace Stegner; Historic newspapers at www.newspapers.com and Utah Digital Newspapers at www.digitalnewspapers.org. "Church of Jesus Christ of Latter-day Saints," by J. Gordon Melton, Britannica, www.britannica.com/topic/Church-of-Jesus-Christ-of-Latter-day-Saints; "Passion and Principle: John & Jessie Fremont," by Sally Denton. "History of the Church of Jesus Christ of Latter-day Saints," www.history.churchofjesuschrist.org.

CHAPTER 14:
DIAMONDS IN THE ROUGH
COUNTRY CREATED 1870s FRENZY

———

In 1872, financial centers in San Francisco, New York and London were abuzz with the news of a great diamond discovery on an isolated mountain in Colorado Territory. There was speculation that diamond mines in South Africa and exchanges in Europe would be eclipsed by the great U.S. discovery.

U.S. government surveyor Clarence King was as astonished as anyone when he first visited the mountain that autumn and spied diamonds unexpectedly lying on the surface. Soon, however, he and his Rocky Mountain survey team made a disturbing discovery: Some of the diamonds were already cut. The diamond field was a hoax. The mountain had been "salted" with low-grade diamonds, some of which had been cut by professional gem cutters.

Salting with gold nuggets was a well-established technique for fooling potential mine investors. But this was new. And the fact that the diamond discovery was in an isolated part of the country added to the allure. The site – now known as Diamond Peak – was in Brown's Park in the far northwest corner of Colorado Territory.

The hoax itself was born more than 1,000 miles away, however. In late 1870, two scruffy-looking prospectors, Philip Arnold and his cousin John Slack, visited financier George Roberts in San Francisco, saying items they had in a rough leather bag needed to be kept safe in a bank. Roberts persuaded Arnold to show him the contents of the bag – uncut diamonds and other gems. But Arnold and Slack were coy about where they found the gems, and they didn't seem interested in financial partners. Nonetheless, Roberts contacted his friend William Ralston, head of the Bank of California. The two recognized a potentially lucrative investment, but they wanted proof.

Faced with constant pressure from the financiers, Arnold and Slack agreed to allow their diamonds to be appraised, and a preliminary estimate of $125,000 was given. The two men then disappeared for several months, returning with more diamonds. The bankers paid them a $100,000 down payment for their claim. It was the first of more than $550,000 that would eventually be paid to the two men. Arnold and Slack also agreed to take some of their diamonds to jeweler Charles Lewis Tiffany in New York to be appraised, then guide a small group to examine the diamond mountain itself. Joining both efforts was a friend of Ralston named Asbury Harpending, who had made a fortune mining in the West and Mexico.

Harpending, Arnold and Slack met Tiffany in New York in 1871, and he valued the sample of diamonds he was given at $150,000. From that, Harpending concluded the leather bag full of gems owned by Arnold and Slack was worth $1.5 million. In New York, the investment group led by Ralston attracted former Civil War General George B. McClellan and Congressman Benjamin Butler. In London, financier Baron Rothschild was eager to invest.

First, however, on-site verification was demanded. So, in the spring of 1872, Harpending, Arnold and Slack traveled to Brown's Park, accompanied by Henry Janin, a preeminent mining expert. Four days of difficult riding from the railroad at Rawlins, Wyoming, took them to the diamond mountain.

"Everywhere we found precious stones – principally diamonds," Harpending wrote. "It was quite wonderful how generally the gems were scattered over a territory about a quarter mile square." After two days, Janin determined "the absolute genuineness of the diamond fields," Harpending said. The group staked a 3,000-acre claim to ensure they got the entire diamond field, then headed home.

Ralston, Roberts, Harpending and others formed the San Francisco and New York Mining and Commercial Co., with 25 founding shareholders putting up $80,000 apiece. They paid Arnold and Slack the remainder of their money, and the two hustlers were out of the diamond business.

News of the diamond find spread rapidly, prompting stories of similar discoveries. Diamond fields were reported in Arizona, New Mexico, Utah and Colorado's San Juan Mountains. Meanwhile, the San Francisco mining company was preparing for a public stock sale of some $10 million in November 1872 when Clarence King dropped his bombshell.

On November 11, according to Harpending, the mining company received a telegram from King "stating that the diamond fields were fraudulent and plainly 'salted.'" A meeting of the board of directors was hastily arranged, and the stock sale was suspended. King, who had arrived in San Francisco, guided some company officials back to the diamond mountain to prove the fraud.

By early December, newspapers across the country, including in Salt Lake City and Denver, were reporting on "The Great Diamond Swindle." Diamond fever evaporated across the West. But one question remained: How did Arnold and Slack trick so many intelligent people?

Arnold, it seems, had worked for a San Francisco drill company that used uncut diamonds for drill bits. He may have acquired his first diamonds there. As the scheme progressed, Slack and Arnold, with money from a previous mining venture, made at least two trips to Europe. They purchased relatively cheap, poor-grade diamonds – some of them already cut – and other gems. It's estimated they spent $20,000 for stones that netted them more than half a mil-

Brown's Park – Brown's Park in Colorado, 1872, as photographed by a member of Clarence King's survey team. *Timothy H. O'Sullivan photograph, Library of Congress.*

lion dollars. They used steel rods to push the gems deep into anthills and other spots on the diamond mountain. They also left gems on the surface in places like rock crevices.

That seemed suspicious to King and his men. So was the fact diamonds were found so close to rubies, sapphires, and other gems, a geologic anomaly that didn't occur anywhere else in the world, so far as King knew. But eager investors ignored these facts as they envisioned a diamond bonanza.

Charles Tiffany was reportedly taken in because he was shown uncut stones, while his expertise as a jeweler was based on professionally cut ones. Mining expert Janin said he believed the diamond field's veracity had been established before he visited. His only mission was to establish the boundaries of the field and estimate its value, he claimed.

The hoax fallout affected the principals differently:

- Harpending lost his initial investment but recovered financially and moved to Kentucky. He was accused of participating in the fraud, but it wasn't proved. He wrote his version of the diamond-hoax story in 1913.

• Ralston paid off all the investors, much of it with his own money. His Bank of California failed in 1875, and Ralston drowned in San Francisco Bay soon thereafter. Many people believe he committed suicide.

• Philip Arnold was sued by several investors for $350,000. He denied he had swindled anyone but agreed to pay $150,000. He opened a bank in Kentucky and died a few years later after being shot by a business rival.

• John Slack disappeared after the hoax, having received little of the diamond money. He died in 1896 in New Mexico.

• Clarence King, hero of the diamond hoax, became a national celebrity and the first head of the U.S. Geologic Survey. But later mining investments destroyed his finances. He died in poverty in Phoenix, Arizona, in 1901.

Sources: "The Great Diamond Hoax and Other Stirring Incidents in the Life of Asbury Harpending," by Asbury Harpending; "The Great Diamond Hoax of 1872," by Robert Wilson, Smithsonian Magazine, June 2004; "The Great Diamond Hoax," by Russell Quinn, Gold! magazine, 1970; Uintah County Regional History Center, Vernal, Utah; Historic Utah and Colorado newspapers at www.digitalnewspapers.org and www.coloradohistoricnewspapers.org.

CHAPTER 15:
HAYDEN CREW CREATED DETAILED
COLORADO MAPS, DESPITE OBSTACLES

———

Long before the 1870s, various groups attempted to map parts of Western Colorado, from Spaniards coming north from New Mexico in the 18th century to early 19th century military and railroad surveys. But it wasn't until the years 1873 through 1876, with the work of Ferdinand V. Hayden and his crews of topographers, geologists, botanists and photographers, that the whole of Colorado was mapped in minute detail.

As maps from the survey were being prepared in 1877, Hayden wrote, "When finished, Colorado will have a better map than any other State in the Union, and the work will be of such a character that it will never need to be done again." He was wrong about the latter claim. Still, the Hayden Survey maps were good enough to be used as the basis for other state maps for decades. Even today, they are surprisingly accurate.

The Hayden Survey was officially known as the "Geological and Geographical Survey of the Territories." Hayden began his government survey work in Nebraska Territory in 1869, then moved to the Yellowstone River region in Wyoming Territory in 1871-1872. His work there helped convince Congress to establish Yellowstone National Park in 1872. In 1873, Hayden moved his crews to Colorado Territory.

Hayden's work was one of four major surveys of the West conducted after the Civil War. John Wesley Powell made two famous trips down the Green and Colorado Rivers in 1869 and 1871-1872 and recorded details of the landscape and people; Clarence King worked on surveys through parts of the Dakotas, Wyoming, Northern Utah, and Colorado; and George Wheeler explored California and Nevada on behalf of the U.S. Army. There was intense competition among survey leaders, both for funding from Congress and for public prestige, at least until 1879, when the U.S. Geologic Survey was established.

All four surveys provided important data, but Hayden's crews conducted the most detailed look at the landscapes they explored, developing topographic contour lines and in-depth reports about the resources available in these areas. The work was done to encourage economic development and to entice railroads, farmers, ranchers, miners, and others to the region. The fact that people already lived in Western Colorado and nearby – primarily Utes, Paiutes and Navajos – was largely ignored. But it caused problems in the 1875 mapping

Mancos Canyon – Captain John Moss and Ernest Ingersoll in the Canyon of the Mancos, Colorado, Hayden Survey, 1874. *William Henry Jackson photo, Library of Congress.*

season.

Hayden divided his survey crews into seven divisions: Three topographic and geologic mapping divisions examined different regions of the state. Each had its own topographer, geologists, mule packers, and a cook. A triangulation division determined high points from which each section would be surveyed. The supervisory division, led by Hayden himself, visited the entire state. A quartermaster division made sure food and other supplies arrived for the field crews at designated supply camps. The photographic division was led by William Henry Jackson, who became famous for his Colorado photographs.

The Middle Division of the three mapping groups – the division responsible for the Grand Valley, Uncompahgre Valley, and as far west as the La Sal Mountains in Utah – was headed by Henry Gannett, topographer, and Albert C. Peale, geologist.

Before the start of the 1875 season, James T. Gardner, head of the Triangulation Division, met with Chief Ouray. The Ute leader warned him about a group of renegade Utes and Paiutes who might attack one or two individual travelers. But Ouray also said that a group of armed men should be safe from the renegades. Many Utes, including Ouray, feared the Hayden Survey's work would be a prelude to white settlement. But the renegades along the Colorado-Utah border were the only ones to physically attack members of the Hayden Survey.

Gardner planned to establish a point on the highest peak in the La Sal Mountains that would allow mapping west to the Colorado River in Utah. He joined his division with the Middle Division mapping group led by Henry Gannett. They met at Gannett's supply camp on the Dolores River near present-day Gateway, Colorado, in early August 1875. On August 7, a group of 13 men left the Dolores camp for the La Sals – six scientists and six hired employees who included mule packers and an African-American cook called Judge Porter. A New York Times reporter named Cuthbert Mills also joined the group. Riding and leading mules, the team arrived at the La Sals on August 11. They spotted nine Indian lodges about six miles east of them.

After two rainy days, during which the surveyors huddled in their tents, nine Indians rode into the surveyors' camp "making signs of friendship and shaking hands," Gardner wrote later. They wanted to trade for tobacco and gunpowder, but the survey party had limited supplies and declined to trade. "We bid them 'adios' and started forward over the hill," Gardner recalled. "No sooner had the rear guard passed the brow than the Indians commenced firing from behind it."

The surveyors hustled their mule train forward as rapidly as possible to get out of rifle range. For the next 24 hours, the Hayden men abandoned their survey equipment and much of their food as they searched for a route out of a deep canyon that would allow them to avoid the renegades' rifles. They finally found it on a treacherous trail up the east side of the canyon late in the afternoon the day after the attack began. Then they rode southeast to the Colorado-Utah border, fearing all the time that the angry Utes were pursuing them. But they were not.

On August 19, they reached Parrot City, a small mining camp near present-day Hesperus, Colorado, having traveled more than 200 miles in five days. "Out of thirty-two animals, we brought off 28 … Not a man was wounded and none are sick," Gardner reported.

Despite the 1875 setback, the survey work continued. Henry Gannett and Albert Peale returned in 1876 to complete their mapping work. This time, they were accompanied by four Ute guides provided by Chief Ouray, and there were no more confrontations.

During three seasons, from 1874 to 1876, the Middle Division mapped more than 15,000 square miles of Western Colorado using only transits, mercury barometers and special telescopes to determine location based on the stars. The maps they produced show topographic contours, river drainages, geologic formations, mineral and agricultural potential, all accompanied by detailed drawings of specific locations. Their written reports also included information about formations that might hold dinosaur fossils; about insects that could prove a problem for agriculturalists; and even about the possible extermination of the American bison.

The other divisions also did critical work. Jackson's photographic division took famous photographs of Holy Cross Mountain and some of the earliest photos of other Colorado landmarks, such as the Royal Gorge. In 1874, the Southern Division, which focused on the San Juan Mountains, mapped approximately four million acres that the Utes had agreed to open for mining under the Brunot Agreement approved earlier that year.

Additionally, in August 1874, Franklin Rhoda, assistant topographer with the Southern Division, recorded the first documented ascent of Mount Sneffels, a 14,158-foot mountain near Ouray, Colorado. The 14-hour round-trip hike was difficult and tiresome for the four men involved, Rhoda reported. "But all our labor was soon rewarded by the glorious view which presented itself to us when we reached the top."

The 360-degree view included the Gunnison River, and to the north, "beyond the Gunnison ... there appeared a very elevated plateau, which ... presented a nearly horizontal profile for a considerable distance." That "nearly horizontal profile" was what we now call Grand Mesa. In 1874, members of the Hayden Survey referred to it as "the great plateau" or "Great Mesa." By 1875, they had settled on the name "Grand Mesa."

Although the Hayden Survey maps and annual reports were incredibly accurate in many respects, the team was not always correct. For instance, the Middle Division initially placed Unaweep Canyon near present-day Delta, Colorado, instead of west of Whitewater Creek. Hayden himself underestimated Colorado's potential. "Colorado will never support so dense a population that a more detailed survey will be required," he wrote in 1877.

Despite such errors, the survey provided detailed maps and reports, and it named important landscape features. In addition to Grand Mesa, Peale and Gannett named Plateau Creek, the Paradox Valley, Divide Creek, the Little Book Cliffs, and the Grand Valley. In one report, Peale noted that the desert area of the Grand Valley might one day "be reclaimed by irrigation from the Grand River." In fact, irrigation from the Grand, or Colorado River, has made the Grand Valley one of the most productive agricultural regions in Colorado.

The survey, with its detailed maps and geological reports, also helped attract the miners, farmers, ranchers, and settlers that Chief Ouray and other Utes feared.

Sources: "Mapping the Four Corners: Narrating the Hayden Survey of 1875," by Robert S. McPherson and Susan Rhoades Neel; "Henry Gannett and Albert C. Peale, Pioneer Mapmakers of the Hayden Survey on the Western Slope," by William L. Chenoweth; : James T. Gardner letters in the Rocky Mountain News, www.coloradohistoricnewspapers. org; Annual reports of "The United States Geological and Geographical Survey of the Territories," by F.V. Hayden; "Geological and Geographical Atlas of Colorado and Portions of Adjacent Territory," by F.V. Hayden; "The Four Great Surveys of the West," www.usgs.gov.

CHAPTER 16:
BUFFALO SOLDIERS PROTECTED SETTLERS
AND UTE INDIANS ALIKE

During a snowstorm in early October 1879, some 35 African-American cavalry troops – Buffalo Soldiers – rushed to aid 150 white soldiers pinned down by Ute Indians at Milk Creek, northeast of present-day Meeker, Colorado. Led by their white commanding officer, Captain Francis Dodge, the members of Company D, U.S. Ninth Cavalry covered approximately 60 miles from Hayden, Colorado, to Milk Creek in 23 hours. When they galloped into the barricades where the white soldiers were hunkered down early on the morning of October 2, any racial animosity that may have existed disappeared. The white troops leaped up to cheer the Buffalo Soldiers and shake their hands.

Amazingly, the Utes who had the white soldiers besieged didn't fire a shot as the Black troopers arrived. Private Caleb Benson, one of the Buffalo Soldiers at Milk Creek, explained years later: "The Indians never shot a colored man unless it was necessary," he said. "They always wanted to win the friendship of the Negro race and obtain their aid in campaigns against the white man."

That may be, but in 1886, when Ninth Cavalry units were sent to serve at new Fort Duchesne on the Ute Reservation in Northeastern Utah, Utes there were horrified. "Buffalo Soldiers! Buffalo Soldiers! We can't stand it! It's bad! Very bad," one Ute leader exclaimed to Eugene E. White, the Indian agent on the reservation. White later said the Utes had "a strange and irreconcilable antipathy to negroes."

It's not clear why the Utes so adamantly objected to the Buffalo Soldiers' arrival at Fort Duchesne. Perhaps it was because many Utes there were originally from Colorado, people who had been forcibly removed to Utah following the 1879 Milk Creek battle and the simultaneous killing of White River Indian Agent Nathan Meeker and his male employees. No doubt many of those Utes recalled the Buffalo Soldiers' involvement at Milk Creek.

In any event, Companies B and F of the Ninth Cavalry arrived at Fort Duchesne in 1886 and helped build its permanent structures. Ninth Cavalry companies were garrisoned there until late 1901. They served as a regional police force, kept white settlers from invading the reservation, and even protected the Utes from angry whites, both in Utah and Northwestern Colorado. In 1898, the Buffalo Soldiers guarded a shipment of government payments for the Indians when rumors spread of a possible robbery attempt by Butch Cassidy's Wild

Maneuvers at Fort Duchesne – Members of the Ninth Cavalry, known as Buffalo Soldiers, on maneuvers at Fort Duchesne, Utah, late 19th century. *Used by permission, Uintah County Library Regional History Center, all rights reserved.*

Bunch. No attempted robbery occurred, however, perhaps because the outlaws weren't willing to attack well-trained soldiers.

African-American soldiers and sailors have served in every United States military conflict, beginning with the Revolutionary War. An estimated 186,000 served during the Civil War, and afterward there was a push to create new units for them. In 1866, Congress passed legislation establishing six new African-American units – four infantry regiments and the Ninth and Tenth Cavalry – all to be commanded by white officers. The cavalry units and two of the infantry were assigned to outposts in the West, where they protected white settlers from hostile Indians, helped track down outlaws, and guarded the border with Mexico.

The Tenth Cavalry first received the nickname "Buffalo Soldiers" from Cheyenne or Comanche Indians, although various stories exist about how this occurred. Some said it was because they wore buffalo coats, or that their curly hair reminded Indians of buffalo hair. More likely are accounts that the Black troopers repeatedly demonstrated their bravery and tenacity in confrontations with Indians, character traits that the Indians ascribed to the buffalo. Soldiers with both the Ninth and Tenth Cavalry accepted the nickname as a sign of respect. The Tenth Cavalry eventually included the buffalo as part of its regimental crest.

Both the Ninth and Tenth served in the Southwest, the Rocky Mountains, and the Great Plains, from Texas to Montana. The Ninth was at Fort Lewis in Colorado – at the fort's first location near Pagosa Springs – when it was sent north to help deal with the Utes at Milk Creek in 1879. The Milk Creek Battle ended several days after the Buffalo Soldiers joined the white soldiers, when more reinforcements arrived and the Utes retreated.

The Buffalo Soldiers in Utah eventually earned the Utes' respect, as well as the respect of many whites in the Fort Duchesne region. White and Black regiments served simultaneously at Fort Duchesne, and often worked together at the fort or on maneuvers outside it. The Black soldiers participated in regional baseball games, band concerts, horse races and holiday celebrations.

But that doesn't mean they avoided the overt racism of the time. In fact, the first white commander of the Buffalo Soldiers at Fort Duchesne was appalled when he was assigned to their unit. Major F.W. Benteen described the Black soldiers as having a "low-down, rascally character." Black soldiers were excluded from many social activities and from the Owl Club, which was organized for white soldiers. There were several confrontations between off-duty Buffalo Soldiers and whites at local saloons.

Still, many of the black soldiers served with distinction. During its service at Fort Duchesne, the Ninth Cavalry included a pair of young Black officers, two of the first three African-Americans to graduate from the U.S. Military Academy at West Point, New York: John H. Alexander and Charles Young. Additionally, a young enlisted man named Benjamin Oliver Davis served with the Buffalo Soldiers at Fort Duchesne from 1899 to 1901. In 1940, Davis became the first African-American general in the U.S. Army.

Tenth Cavalry companies under then-Major John Pershing joined Teddy Roosevelt in the charge up San Juan Hill in Cuba in 1898. Both the Ninth and Tenth served in the Spanish-American War and later in the Philippines. When the Ninth Cavalry units left Fort Duchesne headed for Cuba in 1898 and prepared to board trains in Price, Utah, white citizens of the area, gave them a rousing send-off. There was a luncheon, an integrated baseball game, and children singing patriotic songs.

Together, the Ninth and Tenth Cavalry units served more than a quarter century in the West. Military historian William Leckie summed up their service: "The Ninth and Tenth Cavalry were first-rate regiments and major forces in promoting peace and advancing civilization along America's last continental frontier."

Even so, some who served in the famous regiments had difficult lives after leaving the service. One such man was Sergeant Henry Johnson, who won the Medal of Honor for his bravery during the Milk Creek battle by crawling to the creek to obtain water for wounded men. Johnson remained in the Army until 1898, but he suffered frequent setbacks. He spent time in the stockade and was busted in rank three times. He died in 1904 in Washington, D.C., at a government asylum for the mentally ill.

Grand Junction, Colorado's James Harris had a more pleasant post-military career in Colorado. He was a Buffalo Soldier, but not when the Milk Creek battle occurred. Born to slave parents in Missouri in 1860, Harris enlisted in the Ninth Cavalry in 1882. His first major conflict, as he recalled during a 1938 interview with *The Daily Sentinel*, in Grand Junction, was in 1884 to prevent Sooners from homesteading in Indian Territory in what is now Oklahoma. The Ninth Cavalry rounded up about 300 Sooners and escorted them out of the territory without violence, Harris said.

In 1886, Harris was part of the first group of soldiers assigned to Fort Duchesne. He didn't mention any antagonism from the Utes when he recalled his time there. But he did remember that the first days at the fort were marked by limited rations and inadequate supplies. "We had no shoes for our mounts or the mules that pulled the wagons," he recalled. "General [John] Hatch came over from Fort McKinney and ordered everybody that had any kind of horseshoes to bring them to the quartermaster's blacksmith shop ... I was both a farrier and a blacksmith, so I was kept pretty busy."

After leaving the Army in 1887, Harris lived in Glenwood Springs, Aspen, and Denver, Colorado before moving to Grand Junction in 1900. He married Eva Baylor that same year. The couple had no children, but they led a quiet and apparently comfortable life. They owned a farm near Whitewater for a time. They also bought and sold properties in Grand Junction. Harris worked as a blacksmith in the city, a railroad porter and, in his later years, a janitor in the Mesa County Courthouse. He died in 1943 and is buried at the Orchard Mesa Cemetery in Grand Junction.

Other Buffalo Soldiers retired near where they served. For instance, Caleb Benson, who served at Milk Creek along with Sergeant Johnson, retired near Fort Robinson in Nebraska after a long military career that ended at the Nebraska fort.

Sources: "Hollow Victory: The White River Expedition of 1879 and the Battle of Milk Creek," by Mark E. Miller; "One solder's Service: Caleb Benson in the Ninth and Tenth Cavalry, 1875-1908," by Thomas R. Buecker, Nebraska History magazine, Summer 1993; "The Buffalo Soldiers: Guardians of the Uintah Frontier 1886-1901," by Ronald G. Coleman, Utah Historical Quarterly, Fall 1979; "For Duchesne's Buffalo Soldiers," By Dr. Gary Lee Walker, The Outlaw Trail Journal, Winter 1994; "African American Recipients of the Medal of Honor," by Charles W. Hanna; historic editions of The Daily Sentinel at www. newspapers.com; the Museum of Western Colorado; Orchard Mesa Cemetery, Grand Junction, Colorado.

PART FOUR:
COMMUNITIES

Pioneer ditch builders – Members of the Colorado Cooperative Co. work on the irrigation ditch that would supply water to the community at Nucla, Colorado. *Rimrocker Historical Society of Western Montrose County.*

CHAPTER 17:
INTERNAL DISCORD, NATIVE CONFLICTS
DOOMED FIRST MOAB SETTLEMENT

The first non-Native community in Southeastern Utah, in the valley where Moab now sits, predated all other white settlement in the area by more than 20 years. But it only lasted a few months.

The Elk Mountain Mission, which was named for the Elk Mountains in Utah that are now called the La Sals, was established in 1855 at the behest of the Church of Jesus Christ of Latter-day Saints. However, disputes among the members of the mission, poor leadership, and conflict with Native Americans forced the Mormon pioneers to abandon the settlement.

To reach the Moab Valley, the mission followed a route traversed in 1854 by a scouting party sent out by LDS President Brigham Young. Headed by William Dresser Huntington, the scouting party was to find a place to establish a Mormon presence along the Old Spanish Trail in Southeastern Utah and trade with Natives.

The scouts departed from Springville, Utah, in October 1854 with 13 men, including a Ute guide, a few oxen, horses, and five wagons. They headed southeast to the Green River, then south to the Grand (Colorado) River.

"There is a beautiful valley on the Grand River," Huntington wrote in a letter to the *Deseret News* of Salt Lake City in December 1854. "It has good soil, and grazing range, is very well timbered and watered and is about 50 miles from the Elk Mountains." Huntington's crew camped there briefly, then continued south to the San Juan River, which they called St. John's River, then traveled another 40 miles to a Navajo village in today's Arizona.

They were guided by some friendly Sheberetch Utes – a small band who lived near the La Sal Mountains. The scouting party returned home just before Christmas, and Huntington made an official report to Brigham Young. As a result, Young issued a call for the Elk Mountain Mission for 1855, and 41 men joined.

Alfred Billings, just 29, was chosen as mission president, empowered to act as the military, civil and religious leader for the other 40 missionaries. Oliver Huntington, William's brother, kept the mission's official record, as well as a private journal in which he frequently criticized Billings.

The Elk Mountain Mission left Manti, Utah, on May 22, 1855, with 15 wagons, 65 oxen, 16 cows, 13 horses and other livestock. They also had tools for

Elk Mountain Mission – A monument in downtown Moab, Utah, recognizes the members of the unsuccessful effort to settle the area in 1855. *Robert Silbernagel photo.*

farming, blacksmithing and building. They had abundant black powder, bullet lead, and percussion caps – enough to trade with Natives and still provide for their own weapons.

The initial part of the journey was uneventful, but it took them six days to cross the fast-flowing Green River, using a wagon that converted to a boat. Many of the reluctant oxen had to be tied to the boat and pulled across. The men reached the Grand River on June 10, and though it was also swollen with spring runoff, they got all their livestock and wagons to the south side by June 15. Because it was late in the season, the first order of business was to plant crops. To that end, members of the mission dammed Mill Creek, which now runs through Moab, and they built two miles of irrigation ditch.

But fissures were already appearing. During a meeting June 17, many of the group objected to Billings' plan for a single, communal farming arrangement. Instead, they decided to divide into four separate groups or "messes," each with its own leadership.

Near the end of June, Billings determined to build the mission fort about a mile from the farming plots, in what today is the Scott and Norma Matheson Wetlands Preserve at Moab. The move away from the farm plots further angered some mission members. Even so, a wooden stockade was built, then four separate rock houses – one for each of the messes.

Near the end of June, the first Utes appeared, friendly and willing to be baptized as Mormons. But on June 30, Sheberetch Chief Quit-sub-soc-its, nicknamed St. John by the Mormons, arrived and was angry to find the mission constructing buildings and planting in the valley. Billings appeased the chief by giving him a number of gifts from the mission's trade supplies. Afterward, the Mormons began trading with the Utes at a brisk clip.

Throughout July, other large bands of Natives – Utes and others – arrived at the Mormon fort, curious and eager to trade. They came from all over Western Colorado and Utah, and from Taos and Santa Fe. The Mormons acquired more than 60 good horses, which were in short supply in the Salt Lake Valley, as well numerous, much-sought-after Ute-tanned deer hides.

But not all the Natives were friendly. Chief St. John's brother told the mission members they could not build a permanent fort in the valley. Another Ute said the Mormons had to leave immediately. St. John apparently smoothed things over temporarily, but tensions remained. Utes took some of the Mormon cattle and sheep and helped themselves to the settlers' vegetables. To the Mormons, it was theft. To the Utes, simply part of the price the Mormons paid to occupy their land.

In the midst of this tension, Billings granted 19 mission members leave to visit their homes around Salt Lake. Only four of them returned. Then, on Aug. 31, Billings and five other men, accompanied by five Ute guides, headed south to trade with Navajos. They had a successful journey. But they apparently traded much of their ammunition to the Navajos, leaving themselves short. Also, the trip created more animosity with the Sheberetch Utes, who believed they had exclusive trading rights with the Mormons living in their valley.

A week after Billings and the other traders returned, six more missionaries were allowed to temporarily return to the Salt Lake Valley, leaving only 16 members at the mission.

Four men decided to go hunting in the Elk Mountains (La Sals) on September 22, and several Utes followed them, later killing two of the men, although the reason for the killings is not known. On September 23, while several men were moving livestock near the fort, one was shot by a Ute, and the other Mormons hastily carried him back to the fort. He died that night. Also that night, Utes set fire to a haystack outside the fort and drove off many cattle and horses.

"At daylight the next morning the Indians began to gather round in great numbers," the *Deseret News* reported on October 10. "The remaining 13 brethren, by the advice of some few Indians who were still friendly, took their horses and started for Manti, leaving their enemies quarreling over the cattle and the spoils in the fort."

They hurried north until they reached the Green River, where they felt safer. Most of them arrived at Manti on September 30.

Albert Billings' leadership and his eagerness to trade with the Navajos rather than ensure peace with the Utes have been cited in explaining the Elk Mountain Mission's failure. "It was primarily for the Indian trade that the mission was left vulnerable and hopelessly undermanned," wrote the authors of the book, *The Elk Mountain Mission*. They added, "A stronger, better and more duty-bound mission leader might have produced an entirely different end result."

After the mission was abandoned, Utes kept out other prospective settlers for decades. But by 1880, the Sheberetch Utes had disappeared, devastated by disease and warfare. The few remaining are believed to have joined other Ute bands.

In the late 1870s, when the Utes were mostly gone, new settlers began cautiously moving into the valley. One was an African-American named William Granstaff, who prospected in the area, lived at the abandoned Mormon fort, and ran cattle east of Moab in a place now known as Granstaff Canyon.

Sometime around 1880, the first cabins were built in Moab. One was believed to have been built by Randolph Stewart, the first bishop of Moab, around 1881. However, despite having a bishop, Moab was not an exclusively Mormon community.

"There were Mormons and non-Mormons mixed together right from the first," wrote Richard Firmage in his *History of Grand County*. "Mormons never came to the area en masse as part of a formal settlement from church leaders as they did in most of the other towns of the territory." Many of the early settlers were cattle ranchers, and a few farmers, who arrived from central Utah, Colorado, New Mexico and Texas, he said.

With those settlers, its good water and temperate climate, Moab grew steadily over the ensuing decades, mostly as agricultural community. Then, during the 1950s and 1960s, its population exploded as it became one of the centers for uranium mining and processing. When that economic driver began to evaporate during the late 1970s and 1980s, the community turned more and more toward tourism, which continues to drive the Moab economy in the 21st century.

Sources: "The Elk Mountain Mission: A History of Moab, Mormons, The Old Spanish Trail and the Sheberetch Utes 1854-1855," by Tom McCourt and Wade Allison; "A History of Grand County: Utah Centennial County History Series," by Richard A. Firmage; "Elk Mountain Mission" monument and "The Old Log Cabin" plaque, both at 65 North, 200 East, Moab Utah. Utah Historical Newspapers at www.digitalnewspapers.org.

CHAPTER 18:
LIKE MANY 19TH CENTURY TOWNS,
RAVENSBEQUE SOON DISAPPEARED

In late June 1885, Frank Keyes arrived at the new U.S. Post Office in Ravensbeque, Colorado, and picked up his mail, the first mail delivered at the site. Postmistress Marie deBeque, who was officially appointed to the position on June 29, 1885, said it marked the first regular mail service "up the Grand River" from Grand Junction, Colorado.

Today the trip from Grand Junction to where Ravensbeque once sat – three miles west of what is now the town of De Beque – is little more than a 45-minute jaunt by car. But in 1885, when there was no road through De Beque Canyon, the trip required a rugged journey in one of two directions. One route took travelers west from Grand Junction to Salt Wash at Fruita, then north to the Bookcliffs and a connection to Roan Creek, then southwest to the Colorado River, then called the Grand, and west to Ravensbeque. The second route went east from Grand Junction to Rapid Creek, then on to Plateau Creek. Next it went in a northeasterly direction on a wagon road now known as the De Beque Cutoff, toward Roan Creek, where travelers had to cross the Grand River and follow it west to the small town.

Either route could take several days and require multiple river crossings. In July, 1884, Dr. Wallace A.E. deBeque (he spelled his name with a small "d," while the name of the town used the uppercase "D") and his wife Marie made the trip from Grand Junction to Ravensbeque, where they were building a ranch. It took them three days along the Rapid Creek route, with two riding horses, one riding mule and two pack mules. "We had a hard trip today in the burning sun," deBeque wrote in his diary. "Marie nearly played out and I the same." But, on the third day, he said, "A march of 12 miles brought us, thank Heaven, to the place known as Ravensbeque."

At the time, Ravensbeque was no more than a conglomeration of ranch buildings serving several families, including deBeque's brother, Colonel Robert N. deBeque. The application to the Postmaster General for the Ravensbeque Post Office said it would serve a population of about 150 people, presumably

Wallace deBeque – Portrait of Wallace deBeque, the founder of Ravensbeque and namesake of the town of DeBeque, Colorado. *Image courtesy of the Museums of Western Colorado.*

surrounding settlers.

Wallace deBeque was born in New Brunswick, Canada, in 1841. It isn't known when he moved to this country, but he served in the Second Maine Cavalry during the Civil War. He was wounded and carried a musket ball in his leg the rest of his life. Dr. deBeque married his first wife soon after the war, but she died following the birth of a daughter. He moved to Colorado for his health. Little is known about his early education, but according to his daughter-in-law, he graduated from three different medical schools, the last one being the University of Denver about 1880. By 1881, he was practicing medicine in Fairplay, Colorado, but not enjoying the climate in the high-altitude mining community. He complained of temperatures 40 degrees below zero and snow three feet deep. "This mild Italian climate (?) is more than I can endure," he wrote in his diary.

By 1883, he had left the high country for Grand Junction, which he described as "a straggled out town of boards, adobe and brick." He added, "Its future may be great but its present is not attractive." Friends encouraged him to start a ranch up the Grand River, arguing the outdoor life would improve his health. He did so, but first traveled to Denver, where he married Marie Therese Bonholzer, a widow from Bavaria, on December 23, 1883. They began work on their ranch the following summer. His diary offers insight into their life at Ravensbeque.

- "Our garden (except the corn which the mule ate up) looks very well, considering the late date of planting."

- "Saw a rattlesnake today and killed it. Also saw a mountain lion about 300 yards away, but he ran from me, which saved me the trouble of running from him, as I was wholly unarmed."

- "Ralph Ostrom came out with some venison, which comes very apropos as we were out of meat."

Additionally, deBeque cut cottonwood trees and built a raft. He and Marie used it several times to cross to the southwest side of the Grand River to visit ranchers. It also ferried building materials for the cabin he was constructing. But when deBeque and his brother tried to use the raft to travel downstream to Grand Junction, it did not work. "We had many narrow escapes going through the canon [canyon] and finally abandoned the raft a mile and a half below Plateau Creek," he wrote.

Dr. deBeque also used his medical skills when needed. On one occasion, he said, a man named Maxwell asked deBeque to treat his ailing mother in a cabin on Rifle Creek, about 30 miles northeast of Ravensbeque . It was an all-day trip, made longer by high water. "Crossing Roan Creek I had an awful time," he wrote. "It was a wild torrent. Had to swim my horse. We both came near to going into eternity via the Grand River. Mrs. Maxwell better. I returned home."

Ravensbeque's days as an official Post Office were brief. Wallace deBeque joined several other entrepreneurs, including Henry Rhone, to develop a toll road through De Beque Canyon that opened in 1886 and considerably shortened the travel time to Grand Junction. They also laid out a new town site several miles east of Ravensbeque, which they named De Beque after their partner. Dr. deBeque bought the first lot in the town, and built a home that still stands there. He and his family were the first residents. In May 1888, Marie deBeque filed papers to apply for a new Post Office at De Beque. A few years later, the Denver & Rio Grande Railroad came through De Beque, and it became an important train stop.

Marie deBeque died in 1896, and deBeque remarried, this time to French native Marie Louise de la Villitte. The couple met in Mexico City. They had three children, including Armand deBeque, who lived in the town named for his father until his death in 1998. Wallace deBeque died and was buried in his namesake town in 1930.

The postal records for Ravensbeque and De Beque also hint at other small communities that arose, then changed or disappeared. There was Ferguson, which became Silt. There was Hightower, far up Roan Creek. And there was Orson, 14 miles southeast of Ravensbeque. Even De Beque almost became something else. In 1889, there was a push to change the town's name to Collbran. The effort failed, and that name was applied to a new town near Grand Mesa.

Sources: "Dr. W.A.E. deBeque and His Pioneering at the Townsite of De Beque," by Mrs. W.A.E., deBeque II [daughter-in-law], The Colorado Magazine, September, 1945; "De Beque House," Colorado Encyclopedia, www.coloradoencyclopedia.org; The Museums of Western Colorado; Palisade Historical Society.

CHAPTER 19:
NUCLA'S COOPERATIVE ROOTS
WERE PART OF 19TH CENTURY MOVEMENT

———

In November 1895, *The Altrurian* – newspaper of the Colorado Cooperative Co. that was trying to establish a collective colony in western Montrose County, Colorado – issued a warning to people who might wish to join: "We do not invite any indolent individual, man or woman, that seeks a Colony with the expectation of living easy," the paper said. "We want willing muscle owners that can swing a pick, turn over a rock, cut down a tree, load a wagon, hold a scraper, drive a team and do a thousand and one things."

Before the colony could succeed, *The Altrurian* said, a 17-mile-long irrigation ditch had to be built from the San Miguel River to Tabeguache Park. The park sits on a large bench on the west side of the Uncompahgre Plateau above the San Miguel River, about 40 miles east of the Utah border. No one knew then that it would take another nine years to complete the ditch.

The ditch was completed, however, and irrigation water began flowing into Tabeguache Park in 1904. A town was built at the eastern edge of the park. It was called "Nucla" because colony members believed it would be the nucleus of the entire San Miguel Basin.

The Colorado Cooperative Co. and the town of Nucla were part of a movement that flourished in the second half of the 19th century. The Union Colony at Greeley is Colorado's most famous collective, having been founded in the early 1870s. More collectives developed, especially in the West, after the economic crash of 1893, often with anti-capitalist views.

The Colorado Cooperative Co. was formed in Denver in early 1894, with a location for its colony not yet chosen. Founding members included two state senators, a state engineer and a founder of a statewide farmers' group. In its Declaration of Principles, the company lamented "the present competitive system" under which "only the strong and cunning can 'succeed,' rendering it almost impossible for an honest man or woman to make a comfortable living." Therefore, the declaration said, "We believe in the enactment of laws that will, when enforced, tend to an equalization of production and distribution, as well as an equality in all matters pertaining to 'Life, liberty, and the pursuit of happiness.'"

Colony members purchased stock in the company, and they were to file homestead claims for their own lands in the park. But to get water they had to

Piñon Cottonwood Trestle, c 1900 – A worker drives a wagonload of goods to the Cottonwood Trestle about 1900, a part of the irrigation project to bring water to the Colorado Cooperative community at Nucla, Colorado. *Rimrocker Historical Society of Western Montrose County.*

work for 20 cents an hour on the irrigation ditch, at the colony's sawmill or on roads for the community. For the colony's women, cooking and cleaning for the work crews were expected tasks. Wages weren't paid in cash. Instead, they were offered in "labor certificates" that could be redeemed for water in the ditch or "for anything the Company may have for sale."

Tabeguache Park was chosen as the colony site after one of the founding members, B.L. Smith, toured Colorado and determined that the unoccupied bench above the San Miguel River was perfect. *The Altrurian*, which derived its name from the word "altruism," published a letter from Smith in January 1895 that told of 25,000 to 40,000 acres of arable land in the park. "About 50 percent of the land is covered with black sage brush," he wrote. "but the balance has neither rock nor brush that would stop a plow for miles."

By early 1895, even though the town of Nucla had yet to be established, 20 members of the cooperative company had moved to a camp outside the mining town of Naturita, Colorado, five miles from the future town of Nucla. Most took the train from Denver to Montrose, then travelled by horse and wagon, west over the Uncompahgre Plateau, to the camp. Work on the irrigation ditch began in February 1896. Soon, a new community was created, known as Piñon, about 12 miles east of Naturita along the San Miguel River. A sawmill to process timbers for the project was established nearby. *The Altrurian* and speakers involved with the effort promoted the colony around the country, and many new members joined.

As a child in 1900, Ellen Peterson moved with her family from Minnesota to the colony. A half century later, she wrote a book about the community. In it, she described her first view of Tabeguache Park as the family descended from the Uncompahgre Plateau: "We were coming out of the aspen when we found ourselves out on a point of land that overlooked the entire San Miguel Basin, including the Tabeguache park ... The scene was breathtaking." Peterson's father went to work in the colony's sawmill, while her mother helped cook for the men.

That same year, an ongoing dispute boiled over between colony members who had made the move to the San Miguel Valley, and those still living around Denver. "Denver stockholders especially objected to the aggressive policy of a few of those living at the colony, who said they were endeavoring to freeze them out," a Front Range newspaper reported. A truce was reached, but the dispute continued to cause problems.

In other setbacks, a boiler explosion at the colony's sawmill in 1898 killed two men and injured a third, and sparked a fire that burned most of the mill. It had to be rebuilt to construct trestles for the ditch. Providing sufficient food for members was difficult, even though the colony had its own dairy and gardens. "Food was rationed," Peterson wrote. "There was a shortage of practically everything excepting flour and beans. Even these items could not be bought indiscriminately." Arguments flared over the slow pace of work on the irrigation ditch, and whether the work should be turned over to private contractors.

But life was more than hard work and hardship. Regularly held plays and concerts often attracted people from neighboring communities. Colony members enjoyed dances and taffy pulls. Children attended school in a Piñon boarding house.

Finally, the workers completed the ditch, and water began flowing to Tabeguache Park in 1904. People who had built homes in Piñon dismantled them and hauled them in pieces up the to the park. The Colorado Cooperative Co., once the heart of the collective, eventually became a private entity to manage park water. It continues to do so today.

In 1895, *The Atrurian* had published articles predicting revolution to overthrow America's capitalist system. "The hundreds of co-operative associations that are being organized all over the United States form the one bright star that shines out above the dark horizon of the future," it said. But, after water arrived in Tabeguache Park, and colonists began to build their own farms, the collective aspect of the community gradually disappeared, said Jane Thompson, president of the Rimrocker Historical Society in the San Miguel Basin.

"It was one thing to work side-by-side to build a ditch for the community," she said. "But it was something else to work individually to clear and irrigate your own farm … Certainly, they still had a spirit of cooperation," and they worked together to build a school, church and community buildings in the new town of Nucla.

By 1914, however, the agricultural community with its center at Nucla was much like many other farming communities in Western Colorado.

Sources: The Altrurian, at www.coloradohistoricnewspapers.org; other historic newspapers at www.newspapers.com; "The Spell of the Tabeguache," by Ellen Z. Peterson; Rimrocker Historical Society; "Colorado's Utopian Colonies: Greeley and Nucla," at www.history.denverlibrary.org.

CHAPTER 20:
FIRST GRAND JUNCTION CITY CHARTER
LED NATION IN INNOVATION

In the 21st century, there has been a national effort, not always successful, to adopt an election system called "ranked-choice voting." It is interesting to note that Grand Junction, Colorado, adopted a version of that system early in the 20th century, when its first city charter was approved in September 1909. It may have been the first community in the country to do so.

The Daily Sentinel newspaper in Grand Junction was ambivalent about the new system prior to the September 1909 vote. But two months later, when the first candidates were elected under the charter, and a Socialist won the mayor's spot, the newspaper declared the new voting system the "Offspring of [a] Bone Head."

The man who drafted the 1909 charter – the person the *Sentinel* called a bonehead – was local attorney James W. Bucklin. He included the ranked-choice voting system, which he called preferential voting, as part of the charter. Bucklin later became Grand Junction's city attorney, and in 1911 he penned an article for a national publication in which he said preferential voting, "is a plan to restore majority elections and true representative government." He also claimed the preferential voting system originated in Western Colorado. It was "first formulated in the Grand Junction charter," he wrote.

Preferential voting, or ranked-choice voting, allows each voter to choose his or her No. 1 choice for a particular office, followed by a No. 2 choice and a No. 3 choice (usually no more than three). If no candidate wins more than 50 percent of the vote, the numbers of second-choice votes each candidate received are added to the total. If no one has a majority of votes after that, the third-choice votes are added to the count. Then, the candidate with the most total votes – first, second and third choice – wins.

When Grand Junction adopted preferential voting with its 1909 city charter, political machines affiliated with political parties ran many municipalities. But there was a nationwide effort to curb their powers. Bucklin, writing for *The Annals of the American Academy of Political and Social Science* in November 1911, made it clear that was the intent of the 1909 Grand Junction City Charter. "Political machines are only able to control by minority government. Minority government is bad government," Bucklin wrote. "If then we are to establish good government, we must enact some electoral system that will destroy polit-

Photo to the left: Bucklin – James W. Bucklin, the Grand Junction attorney, and later city manager, who wrote and promoted the 1909 City Charter for Grand Junction, Colorado. *Image courtesy of the Museums of Western Colorado.*

ical machines, and prevent the election of officials by minorities." He added, "Every effort was made by its authors to make our charter democratic, the most democratic in America."

It wasn't just preferential voting that made the charter different. It also established new rules for how city franchises were granted in order to break what Bucklin described as a racket operated by special interests. Additionally, to reduce crime, the new city charter outlawed the numerous saloons in the city. In fact, according to reports in the *Sentinel*, the anti-saloon faction, also called the church faction, was the driving force behind the charter. Liquor would remain prohibited within Grand Junction's city limits for the next 24 years, until Prohibition was repealed nationwide in 1933.

The 1909 charter also established a system of five elected city commissioners, each overseeing a different aspect of municipal operations. The Commissioner of Public Affairs also served as the mayor, but he was not the "boss" of the other commissioners, Bucklin wrote. In addition, there was a Commissioner of Water and Sewers; Commissioner of Finance and Supplies; Commissioner of Highways; and a Commissioner of Health and Civic Beauty.

Five candidates vied for mayor in November 1909, including William H. Bannister, who founded the Bannister Furniture store that operated for 102 years in Grand Junction. Bannister "led all other candidates for first choice in the number of votes received," the *Sentinel* noted. He also led when second-choice votes were tallied, but he still didn't have a majority of total votes cast. Therefore, "it was necessary, according to the new system of voting, to add the third-choice votes to secure the election of a candidate," the *Sentinel* said. When that was done, the victorious candidate was Socialist Thomas Todd, an outcome that surprised nearly everyone. "It's a sure bet that the 'father of the charter' [Bucklin] never anticipated (nor did the church contingent) that Thomas Todd would be elected mayor," said the *Sentinel*.

Bucklin offered a considerably different view of Todd's victory than the *Sentinel*, when he wrote his article for the political science magazine: "For mayor, Mr. Bannister received a plurality of first choice votes, although [he was] an anti-charter candidate, and under the old method of plurality election, would have been elected mayor, although three other candidates received more [total] votes than he," Bucklin wrote. "Under the old plan he would thus have beaten the majority, defeated the will of the electors, and would have represented not the majority, but only a reactionary minority," Bucklin added. "The superiority of the Grand Junction system of preferential voting was thus absolutely and clearly demonstrated."

As a political movement, socialism was familiar to Grand Junction residents before Todd was elected as mayor in 1909. In 1908, Eugene V. Debs, the Socialist Party of America nominee for president, had stopped in Grand Junction. According to the *Sentinel*, more than 1,000 people gathered at the Park Opera House to hear Debs speak, "one of the greatest audiences that ever turned out to hear a political speaker in Grand Junction."

Thomas Todd was installed as mayor late in 1909. In January 1910, a national magazine called *Human Life* published a lengthy article about Todd. The article called Todd "a mayor without a party," because the city charter adopted by Grand Junction in September of 1909 didn't allow party affiliations to be claimed for municipal elections.

Although the *Sentinel* opposed Socialism, it didn't object to Mayor Todd's tenure initially. However, when Todd and the other city commissioners appointed Socialist Sheppard B. Hutchinson as police chief in late November 1911, the *Sentinel* was not pleased. On December 1, 1911, the newspaper said Grand Junction had "the first and only socialist chief of police in the United States." The newspaper also objected strongly to a plan developed by Todd and Chief Hutchinson to create a municipal woodpile, where unemployed men could chop wood and earn food. When the city, under Todd's leadership, tried to gain control of the local electric company to make it a municipal utility and sought to establish a city-owned coal mine for the benefit of workers, the *Sentinel's* opposition to Todd's tenure only grew.

It's not clear when Todd, an Illinois native, became a Socialist. But after his 1909 election, he began to gain national recognition. By 1912, he was even considered as a running mate for Eugene Debs. He lost that bid to the former Socialist mayor of Milwaukee, Wisconsin. Todd decided not to seek re-election to the Grand Junction City Council in November 1913, and later became president of the Grand Junction Chamber of Commerce, with the *Sentinel's* support. The City Charter drafted by James Bucklin remained in effect until 1921, when it was amended to establish the city manager form of government that is still used by the city in the 21st century. Also in 1921, preferential voting was eliminated in the city.

Sources: "The Grand Junction Plan of City Government and Its Results," by James W. Bucklin in "The Annals of the American Academy of Political and Social Science," November, 1911, through www.jstor.org; historic editions of The Daily Sentinel through www.newspapers.com; author interview with Grand Junction City Attorney John Shaver; "Walter Walker and His Fight Against Socialism," by Jeannette Smith, Journal of the Western Slope, Fall, 1997; "When Grand Junction Had a Socialist Mayor," by Noel Kalenian, www.mesacountylibraries.org.

CHAPTER 21:
DECEPTION FOLLOWED A DEATH
AT UTAH SPIRITUAL ENCLAVE

———

When Edith Peshak died near Monticello, Utah, on February 11, 1935, her passing didn't cause an immediate commotion. For one thing, her family and friends didn't believe she was actually dead. Within a few months, however, Peshak's death and the unusual treatment of her remains prompted official inquiries. It also cast an unwelcome light on the community where she lived, known as the Home of Truth or the Ogden Center, and on Marie Ogden, the community's mystic founder.

Initially, Ogden convinced her followers that Peshak wasn't dead. Rather, she was in a sort of limbo from which she would be resurrected, Ogden claimed. Twice a day, two of the 15 colony members gave Peshak's body salt baths to keep it clean and preserved, along with milk enemas, ostensibly to provide nourishment and replace dead cells with live tissue.

Word of Peshak's death reached authorities that spring. In May, the San Juan County sheriff visited, asking to see the body. Ogden refused. With an order from Utah's attorney general, the San Juan County attorney visited and also was turned away. Finally, a local doctor was allowed in, accompanied by two nurses. One nurse later described seeing a corpse, "well preserved and very clean. She has skin stretched over small bones with no muscle or fat, as she had died of cancer." Because there was no state law requiring burial of a corpse if it didn't pose a health hazard, no legal action was taken.

However, news of Peshak's death and the body's preservation made national headlines. Many stories ridiculed the Home of Truth and its founder. More stories appeared two years later when Peshak's son demanded a death certificate for his mother, and Ogden eventually agreed.

Also in 1937, a former colony member filed an affidavit saying that Ogden had instructed him to secretly cremate Peshak's body. Ogden told other group members that the body had been "spirited away from curious and prying eyes." Some members became disenchanted with Marie Ogden, and the community dwindled to about 10 members. Peshak's husband, Elmer, remained.

Such activities were likely surprising to those who knew Marie M. Ogden as a socially active New Jersey housewife prior to 1929. She served on multiple committees, including women's clubs, music foundations and welfare projects, but was not particularly religious.

Marie Ogden as a young woman, at her typewriter. Photo taken prior to her arrival in Utah." *Credit: San Juan County (Utah) Historical Commission.*

In 1929, however, when her husband Harry died of cancer, Marie Ogden began seeking a more spiritual life, investigating astrology, numerology and more. She became associated with William Dudley Pelley, an author, spiritualist, fascist, and anti-Semite who claimed to receive instructions from an oracle on how to live a moral life. Ogden donated at least $12,000 to him. A decade later, when Pelley was convicted and imprisoned for his leadership of a fascist paramilitary organization, Ogden claimed they had never been close.

In 1931, as she was turning away from Pelley, Ogden began receiving her own divine instructions. "We followed a very definite form of Divine Guidance," she wrote. "Messages of Dawn, Truth and Wisdom were relayed from the Higher Realms." The divine advisers guided her fingers as she sat at her typewriter, she said, and later "directed us to come to this western land."

Describing Ogden's spiritual beliefs is difficult, because she was not always clear about them. However, she told an interviewer in 1946 that her group followed "The Aquarian Gospels of Jesus Christ," a mixture of conventional Christianity, metaphysical ideas and reincarnation theories that were created in 1908.

Historian and Western author Wallace Stegner visited the Home of the

Truth in 1940, and wrote that Marie Ogden "controls and directs the community with the aid of messages from the spirit world and from Jesus Christ. The messages come to her upon a hill near her house, and she takes them down on her typewriter."

While still in New Jersey, Ogden reportedly received apocalyptic messages telling her that large cities would soon be destroyed and a new community was needed in the remote West. She initially considered Idaho, Oregon, and California. But she chose Southeastern Utah after another woman claimed she had a divine inspiration and wrote to Ogden describing the area. Ogden and founding members of the Home of Truth arrived near Monticello in September 1933 and initially set up a tent community. They called the area Rainbow Valley, but it is better known as Dry Valley, between Monticello and Moab, Utah, near Church Rock.

At the Inner Portal, the center of the Home of the Truth compound, "there is nothing to detain you but the view, a good one out across the Abajo Mountains – the view and the realization that you now stand on the one spot where you would be safe if the last days should come suddenly," Stegner wrote.

In May 1934, Ogden purchased the *San Juan Record* newspaper in Monticello. She continued to print local news in it, but she also published columns about the Home of Truth. At first, neighbors accepted Ogden's group. "The members, since their coming here, have proven themselves to be people of culture and learning and in all their contacts with the public have created a most favorable impression," a Moab newspaper reported in 1934.

That changed with the Peshak scandal. Newspapers began to refer to the colony as "strange" or "a cult," and termed Ogden a "cultist" and "dictator." Some accused colony members of being lay-abouts, who depended on new recruits' money to sustain them. Ogden angrily disputed that. She said more than 200 people who had arrived to join the colony dropped out because they couldn't handle the hard work it required. The men and women who remained toiled at farming, constructing buildings, and even developing a gold mine.

Stegner reported that Ogden demanded members donate all income to benefit the community, switch to a semi-vegetarian diet, abstain from alcohol and even abandon gardening at one point and instead seek wages as day laborers to purchase food.

In July 1936, another scandal rocked the colony when authorities tried to find 13-year-old Thelma Moss. Her mother and stepfather had joined the colony and had brought Thelma with them. Soon after their arrival, Thelma wrote to her biological father, saying that she was "unhappy and afraid" at the colony. Her dad traveled from Idaho to retrieve her, but he found her gone. The girl had left with her stepfather's brother.

In October 1936, Ogden told a Salt Lake City newspaper there was nothing to worry about. Thelma Moss and her stepuncle "were married and all the family is now happily reunited in Oakland," she said. "The parents gave consent to marry." Ogden didn't say how the man's other wife felt about the marriage. Police said the man had a wife living in Monterey, California, with their children. There was no indication they were divorced.

The Home of the Truth had shrunk to seven members by 1940, despite Ogden's continued predictions of the "doom of civilization" and, consequently, her anticipation that the colony would grow exponentially. That was when Stegner briefly visited the compound, although he didn't meet Ogden. He spoke with a member of the spiritual group named Daisy Naden. When he asked how many colonists there were, Daisy's eyes clouded. "Not everyone is fitted for the great work," she told Stegner. "Many have come and gone, because the sacrifices demanded are great, and too many put materialistic and selfish desires above the sanctification of their lives and persons."

Stegner noted the rugged country and isolated location of the Home of the Truth. He added, "The wilderness has always had a double attraction to the founders of religious cults: it is closer to God, and farther from man."

In a 1946 interview, Ogden was asked about Peshak, but she still declined to say much. "That is one thing that we have been misrepresented in and misquoted on," she said. " We aren't ready to talk about it now … I have all my records and someday we'll tell that story."

But that public telling of Ogden's side of the Peshak story never occurred. Ogden sold the *San Juan Record* in 1949. She worked for years on a book to tell the story of the Home of Truth and presumably Edith Peshak. But when she died at a senior facility in Blanding, Utah, in 1975, one of her few remaining followers burned most of her papers, including, apparently, the manuscript. The land on which the Home of the Truth colony was once located was abandoned by the last of the colony holdouts in 1977.

Sources: "The Home of the Truth: The Metaphysical World of Marie Ogden," by Stanley J. Thayne, master's thesis at Brigham Young University, at www.academia.edu; "Mormon Country," by Wallace Stegner; "Marie Ogden and San Juan County's Home of Truth," by Andrew Gulliford, San Juan Record, June 20, 2017; "Home of Truth Cooperative Settlement" booklets, by Marie Ogden, at University of Utah, J. Willard Marriott Digital Library, www.collections.lib.utah.edu; Utah historical newspapers at www.digitalnewspapers.org.

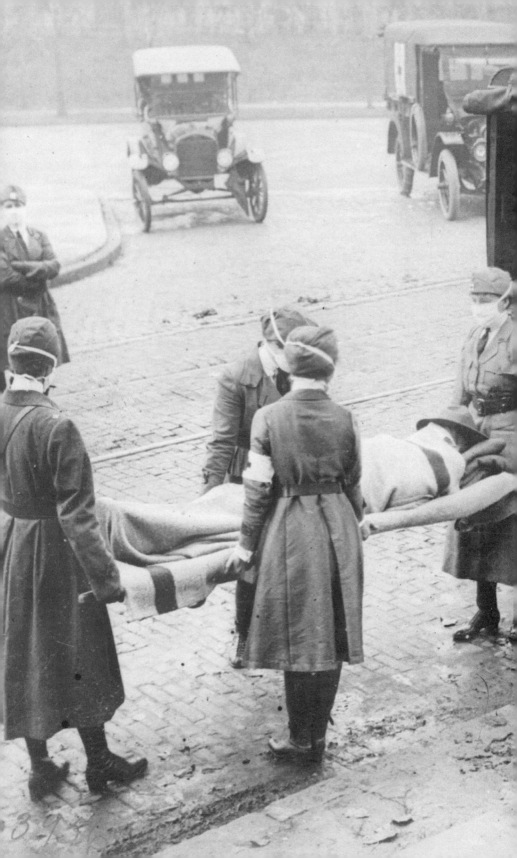

CHAPTER 22:
COMMUNITIES IN COLORADO, UTAH
STRUGGLED TO CONTAIN SPANISH FLU

By late September 1918, as news from the Great War in Europe signaled the conflict's end was near, an ominous article appeared in *The Daily Sentinel* in Grand Junction, Colorado. "First death of influenza in Colorado," the headline read. A Chicago woman had died while visiting Denver. "No other cases have been reported to the health authorities," the article concluded.

Tragically, that wouldn't be true for long. By early November 1918, the *Sentinel* reported nearly 33,000 cases of the disease in Colorado and 1,069 deaths. The influenza epidemic that began in 1918 – the so-called Spanish Flu – eventually killed millions of people worldwide. Exactly how many cases and deaths occurred in Western Colorado and Eastern Utah is not clear. On October 23, while the epidemic was still at its peak, the *Sentinel* said there had been of 171 cases of influenza and related pneumonia in the area. The number of deaths wasn't reported, although the *Sentinel* often carried headlines of flu deaths such as: "Sallie Gilmer is Third Victim of Influenza," and "Two Are Dead and Another Dying in A Palisade Family."

In Utah in late October, the Moab newspaper reported 60 coal miners stricken with the disease in tiny Sego, Utah. Dozens were falling ill in Moab and Monticello, as well.

Reading news about the flu was like riding a roller-coaster. On October 7, a Salt Lake City newspaper said, "Epidemic believed to have run its course." But three days later, the Utah State Board of Health closed all schools, churches, theaters and public gatherings to slow the spread of the disease. In Grand Junction on October 10, doctors claimed the epidemic was "well under control." But on October 23, the *Sentinel* reported there was "much disease" throughout the area. On Monday, October 14, people read that Grand Junction schools, which had been closed earlier in the month, would reopen that Friday. They didn't reopen until late November.

The disease spread rapidly in Colorado and Utah, and communities took drastic actions to curtail it. Silverton, Colorado, had 500 cases of flu and 56

Photo on previous pages: 1918 On Duty St. Louis – St. Louis Red Cross Motor Corps on duty, St. Louis, Missouri, October, 1918. *Library of Congress.*

deaths, the *Sentinel* reported on October 28. To prevent such an outbreak in their community, officials in Montrose County, Colorado, posted armed guards near the county's southern border to turn back any travelers from Silverton or Ouray, Colorado. Delta County, Colorado, officials issued a county-wide quarantine. The penitentiary at Cañon City, Colorado, refused to accept new prisoners because it had so many flu cases.

In Gunnison, Colorado, county physician Dr. F.P. Hanson ordered barricades and fences erected on all main highways near the county borders. Railroad passengers were closely monitored. They could only disembark in Gunnison if they agreed to a four-day quarantine at a hotel in the town.

In Moab, Utah, all travel in and out of the city was prohibited, "unless absolutely necessary." Those who arrived in the city had to spend four days in quarantine.

The disease also attacked Native communities. More than 60 Ute Indians died on the Ouray Reservation near Dragon, Utah, including Chief Atchee, a neighbor of Ute leader Chipeta. Newspaper accounts estimated that 2,000 to 3,000 Navajos died of the disease.

Elsewhere in the country, the flu epidemic was so calamitous it's difficult to imagine, even in the wake of the 21st century's COVID 19 pandemic.

- 85,000 cases in Massachusetts in August and September.
- In New York City, 5,000 people died in one month.
- In Philadelphia, 1,000 bodies awaited burial, but there were no grave diggers to be found.
- Nationwide, 6,200 flu victims died in one week, 675,000 over two years.

Nobody knows where the disease originated. Some researchers said France, Germany, or Asia. A small town along the Kansas-Colorado border has also been suggested. It is known that the first cases *diagnosed* as this strain of influenza were reported in San Sebastián, Spain, in February, 1918. Hence the name, Spanish Flu. It marched through Europe that spring, affecting troop movements on both sides. But few people died in the first wave. Victims usually suffered several days of high fever, chills and aches, then recovered.

However, in August 1918, a second wave appeared, killing millions in India, Japan, China, the Caribbean and South America. The second wave arrived in the United States aboard a troop ship that docked in Boston Harbor in late August. Ten days later there were three flu-related deaths. Nearby Fort Devens became ground zero for the raging influenza. Overcrowded with 45,000 men, by late September the fort averaged 100 flu deaths *per day*. Young soldiers often reported to doctors in the morning with a fever, and were dead before the day was over.

The flu accompanied troops on the move during and after the Great War

1918 Red Cross Ambulance – The Red Cross Emergency Ambulance Station of the District of Columbia, autumn, 1918. *Library of Congress.*

and rapidly spread across the globe. By the end of the epidemic, it's estimated that 20 million to 100 million people had died. Because record keeping was poor or nonexistent in many regions where it struck, exact numbers are impossible. However, even the lower death estimates mean there were more influenza deaths than the 15 million soldiers, sailors and civilians killed in all four years of World War I. No other disease, including the Black Plague, has killed so many people so quickly as the Spanish Flu. And, unlike other epidemics, this one struck healthy young adults – soldiers, sailors, nurses – more than the elderly or very young. For comparison, COVID 19 killed an estimated 6.3 million people globally through June 2022.

The first Spanish Flu death in Mesa County, Colorado, occurred on October 6, 1918, when "Mrs. Emma Smith-Mills of Fruitvale passed away … of the dreaded malady," according to the *Sentinel.* Two days after Smith-Mills died, the Mesa County Board of Health ordered all "schools, churches and other public meeting places" closed to stop its spread. The American Red Cross opened an emergency hospital in Grand Junction on October 31. In early November, the hospital's director sent a letter to the *Sentinel,* pleading with local women to volunteer at the hospital, arguing it was safe if they took appropriate precautions such as wearing masks.

It was a horrific few months, but by the end of 1918, things were returning to normal. The emergency hospital closed just before the new year, having treated 113 flu patients, 28 of whom died. In Salt Lake City and other parts of Utah, flu restrictions were also lifted in late 1918 or early 1919. Moab lifted its quarantine on January 31, 1919. Flu stories began to disappear from newspapers, and the epidemic seemed to evaporate as quickly as it had arrived. There was a third, less serious wave later in 1919, and some cases continued into 1920. But for the communities of Western Colorado and Eastern Utah, the worst was over.

Sources: "Flu: The Story of the Great Influenza Pandemic of 1918," by Gina Kolata; "How the Horrific 1918 Flu Spread Across America," by John M. Barry, Smithsonian Magazine, November 2017. "Gunnison Colorado: the town that dodged the 1918 Spanish Flu pandemic," by Rory Carroll, The Guardian, March 1, 2020; Colorado Historic Newspapers at www.coloradohistoricnewspapers.org and www.newspapers.com; Utah Historic Newspapers at www.digitalnewspapers.org.

PART FIVE:
CHARACTERS

Dempsey Willard – Jack Dempsey lands a right to jaw of Jess Willard during the 1919 fight that won Colorado native Dempsey the title of Heavyweight Champion of the World. *Pulitizer Publishing Company, Library of Congress.*

CHAPTER 23:
FRUITA'S FIRST DOCTOR WAS
AN INNOVATOR AND INVENTOR

———

At the turn of the 20th century, Fruita, Colorado, was a small town bustling with innovation:

- The first electric automobile arrived in town, not from a far-away dealer but through the craftsmanship of local men.
- The first observatory was built at a Fruita home, with a locally constructed telescope.
- Early experiments in using radiation to treat cancer were conducted.
- A company was formed to construct and sell X-ray machines.
- A small hospital was built to serve railroad workers and others.
- The town's first pharmacy opened.

Amazingly, one man was involved in all these endeavors: Dr. James M.G. Beard.

Born in New Hampshire in 1844, Beard taught school in Indiana prior to attending the University of Michigan, then medical schools in Kansas City and Chicago. He practiced medicine in Indiana, Arkansas, Kansas, and Saguache, Colorado, before to moving to Fruita in 1894. Beard and his first wife, Roseltha, had four children. But she died while the family was living in Saguache, and he married his second wife, Mary Ellis, who was known as Mait.

Beard's son, John, joined his father in the creation of Beard and Sons Drugstore. Later, John founded the Beard family's goat and sheep ranch that operated in the Devil's Canyon area of what's now the Bureau of Land Management's McInnis Canyons National Conservation Area southwest of Fruita. Another son, Edgar, published two early newspapers in Fruita.

In 1903, according to *The Daily Sentinel*, in Grand Junction, Colorado, Beard and his son, John, purchased an automobile, which the *Sentinel* described as "the first to be owned in the valley." Because he understood electricity, Dr. Beard decided he wanted an electric automobile, so he had one built. It's not clear how much Beard was involved in its design. But it is known that his friend and neighbor George Newbury, described as a mechanical genius, built the vehicle. Beard drove it around Fruita for several years.

Beard also partnered with Newbury to build a telescope and observatory

Dr. James M.G. Beard – A portrait of Dr. James M.G. Beard of Fruita, an inventor and innovator, as well as a physician in Fruita, Colorado. *Courtesy of Sheila Beard Latte.*

at his home near McCune Avenue in Fruita. It may have been the first observatory in the Grand Valley. Beard ordered the lenses for the telescope himself but returned the first set because they were marred with spots. "I'm not buying a glass map of the Hawaiian Islands," he reportedly said. "I want clear glass for lenses for a telescope." In the 1970s, long after Beard's death, the six-inch telescope was donated to the Delta County School District in Delta, Colorado.

Around the turn of the century, Beard became interested in radiation to treat cancer patients and in radiography, or X-rays. Both fields were in their infancy. Beard reportedly traveled to Unaweep Canyon, southwest of Grand Junction, and mined small amounts of uranium ore, which he ground up and glued into small discs for making radiography images of patients. According to several accounts, he corresponded with Nobel Laureate scientist Marie Curie in Paris about using radioactive substances.

However, his practical mind became dissatisfied with the existing technology for X-ray machines. He turned once again to his friend Newbury. They designed and patented a hand-crank electric system for Beard's X-ray machine. By 1902, Newbury and Beard had established a small manufacturing firm to build and sell the machines. Newspaper articles during this time often reported that other doctors from around the Grand Valley and from other parts of Western Colorado took their patients to Beard for X-rays to diagnose difficult cases. Many area physicians purchased their own X-ray machines from Beard. Later, son John Beard worked with Newbury to build and sell the machines. However, changing technology soon made the design of their X-ray machine obsolete.

Early in the 20th century, Dr. Beard established Fruita's first hospital, a four-bed facility on the second floor of the building that also housed his medical practice. It was near the family drugstore. Working under contract with both the Denver & Rio Grande Railroad and the Uintah Railway, Beard created the hospital primarily to treat railroad workers. But it was also open to local patients. Beard operated the hospital in partnership with Dr. Robert Benjamin Porter, but the facility closed after Beard's death in 1912.

His death is believed to be related to Beard's years-long research into radioactive materials and his extensive handling of them. His X-ray machines had open X-ray tubes, known to be a health risk a few decades later. Obituaries in local newspapers told of Dr. Beard's lengthy fight with an unknown disease. He traveled to the Mayo Clinic in Rochester, Minnesota, to seek help, but doctors there could do little to halt his disease. He died at his home in Fruita on April 27, 1912. But Beard's legacy and family continued in the Fruita area.

In addition to his son John's work at the drugstore and with the X-ray machines, he served for a time as Fruita's town marshal. He and his son Irving later ran angora goats, then sheep in the area from Devil's Canyon to Pollock Canyon southwest of Fruita, as well as on Glade Park and on Piñon Mesa. Irving and his wife, Dorothy, also had ranch property near Leadville and Fairplay, Colorado. John's other son, Wallace Beard, owned and operated a construction company near Fruita for many years. Edgar Beard, John's brother, operated first *The Fruita Independent* newspaper, and later *The Fruita Record.*

Sources: Information from Sheila (Beard) Latta; "Profile of Dr. J.M.G. Beard," by Dorothy Beard, in "Echoes of A Dream;" "Images of America: Fruita," by Denise and Steve Hight; Historic newspapers at www.coloradohistoricnewspapers.org and www.newspapers.com.

CHAPTER 24:
'GLAMOROUS' BULKELEY WELLS
WAS A TYRANT TO TELLURIDE MINERS

———

On January 4, 1904, a headline in *The Daily Sentinel* in Grand Junction, Colorado, blared the news from San Miguel County, Colorado: "Martial Law Declared at Telluride." A mine strike that began the previous October had deteriorated into open warfare. At the center of the dispute was a man named Bulkeley Wells, manager of the Smuggler-Union Mining Co. and leading citizen of Telluride, Colorado. For a time in 1904, Wells was virtual dictator of San Miguel County.

Wells was called "a man of rare courage." It was said he "had a keen sense of justice" and was "a glamorous man." He was handsome, played polo, and would become president of state and national mining organizations. He served on the Colorado Railroad Commission and was a leader in Republican political circles. At the height of the labor battles, when Captain Bulkeley Wells was military commander overseeing martial law, 100 Telluride citizens signed a petition proclaiming their appreciation for Wells's leadership.

But a Socialist Party pamphlet that backed the miners described Wells as "a gentleman and a savage." One union attorney sarcastically referred to him as "the Poo-Bah of San Miguel County." Those who objected to his actions attacked him physically as well as verbally, and he survived an assassination attempt.

Wells was born in Chicago in 1872 and graduated from Harvard University in 1894. In 1895, he married Grace Daniels Livermore, whose father, Colonel Thomas Livermore of Boston, owned a company that purchased the Smuggler-Union Mining Co. in 1899. Wells was named vice president of the Smuggler-Union, and he began visiting Telluride in 1901, just as the labor issues were coming to a head. He later moved there with his wife and young family.

By then, Telluride Miners' Union No. 63, an affiliate of Western Federation of Miners, had declared a strike against the Smuggler-Union because the company refused to accept an eight-hour workday for its employees. The strike lasted several months.

Telluride wasn't the only place where union unrest occurred. Strikes during the early years of the 20th century also led to violence in Cripple Creek, Victor and Idaho Springs, Colorado, and in other states such as Utah and Idaho.

Bulkeley photo – A portrait of young Bulkeley Wells. *History Colorado – Denver Colorado.*

In Telluride, gunfire broke out between union members and scab miners on July 3, 1901. Two scabs and one union man were killed. More than a year later, in November 1902, Smuggler Mine manager Arthur Collins was murdered at his house east of Telluride.

On September 1, 1903, the Telluride Miners Union called a second strike against the Smuggler-Union, as well as the Tomboy and Liberty Bell mills. In late October, Wells and other mine company representatives met with Colorado Governor James Peabody, who, on November 20, ordered National Guard troops to Telluride under the command of Major Zeph Hill.

On January 3, 1904, Peabody declared martial law in San Miguel County, and Hill's soldiers immediately arrested 50 men at the union hall and placed them on a train bound for Ridgway, Colorado, northeast of Telluride. A week later, at Major Hill's request, Bulkeley Wells established Troop A, First Squadron Cavalry, of the Colorado National Guard, made up of Telluride citizens. Wells was elected captain. He would later become a brigadier general.

On February 21, 1904, Major Hill returned to Denver and Wells became military commander of San Miguel County. He restricted freedom of assembly, closed gambling halls, and censored the press and telegraph dispatches. But less than a month later, Peabody lifted martial law and deported strikers began returning. On March 14, 1904, angry townsmen led by Wells ransacked saloons, brothels, and miners' homes in search of union members. Seventy men were deported to Ridgway.

Ten days later, Peabody reinstated martial law and sent Brigadier General Sherman Bell, leader of the Colorado National Guard, to Telluride with 300 troops. In late March, Western Federation of Miners President Charles Moyer and his lieutenant, Big Bill Haywood, were arrested in Ouray on charges of desecrating the flag. Haywood was soon released, but Moyer was transported to Telluride and jailed. During a court hearing March 29, Moyer was released on bond for the criminal charges. But Bulkeley Wells was waiting outside the courtroom and immediately took Moyer into military custody.

A few days later, Judge Theron Stevens in Montrose, Colorado, ordered a writ of habeas corpus for Moyer and demanded he be brought before his court. Wells and General Bell refused to release Moyer, and Bell reportedly responded: "Habeas corpus be damned. We'll give 'em post mortems." Consequently, the judge ordered the arrest of Bell and Wells, but when the Ouray County sheriff traveled to Telluride to enforce Steven's order, Bell and Wells simply refused to be arrested. They were acting in a military capacity under the orders of Governor Peabody, they said, and therefore were not subject to civilian authorities.

On April 16, General Bell withdrew his state troops and left Wells once more in charge of San Miguel County. Shortly afterward, Wells accompanied Moyer to Denver for a hearing on the writ of habeas corpus. But when the train arrived in Denver, there was more violence – this time between Wells and Big Bill Haywood. Depending on which newspaper account one believes, either Haywood attacked Wells with little provocation and knocked him to the floor, or Wells attempted to stop Haywood from speaking with Moyer and Haywood responded by knocking Wells down, whereupon National Guardsmen beat Haywood "into insensibility." Both men soon recovered, and Moyer remained in Wells' custody.

In early June, as Moyer's legal team prepared to take the matter to federal court, Governor Peabody suddenly had a change of heart. He ordered Wells to release Moyer and to have his National Guardsmen stand down. He declared the insurrection in San Miguel County had ended. On November 29, 1904, the strike was officially called off when Wells agreed to institute $3-a-day pay for eight-hour workdays at all Smuggler-Union facilities.

However, the labor issues weren't over for Wells. In early 1907, while accompanying Steve Adams to Idaho where Adams was involved in an unrelated case, Wells supposedly heard Adams' confession to the 1902 murder of Arthur Collins in Telluride. Adams returned to Colorado to stand trial in 1908. But three months before the trial began, there was an attempt to assassinate Wells. Six sticks of dynamite were placed under his bed, with a fuse running out the window. When the dynamite exploded Wells was "hurled against the ceiling and alighted on the opposite side of the room," according to one newspaper account. He suffered cuts and bruises to his face and head. No one was arrested for the attempted killing.

His injuries notwithstanding, Wells was the star witness in Steve Adams' July 1908 trial for Arthur Collins's murder, which was held in Grand Junction. But his testimony wasn't enough. Adams was acquitted, much to the dismay of Wells and other mine owners.

Wells returned to Telluride, where he remained an important citizen. But in the coming years, his life gradually began to unravel. A plan to bring irrigation water and railroad service to a large tract of desert land west of Telluride, in which Wells was a major investor, went nowhere.

In January 1918, Colonel Livermore, the man who had brought Wells to the Smuggler-Union, died. Four months later, Wells's wife divorced him, claiming her husband had deserted her. She left with their four children. Wells's connections to the Smuggler-Union company were eroding. Fire destroyed his home near Telluride in 1920, and in 1923 he left the company and Colorado. That year, he married a woman named Virginia Schmidt, and they lived in California. But she also left him and was living in Arizona with her two children by May 1931.

That's when Wells killed himself in his San Francisco office. He left a note for a longtime friend, saying his money was gone and he feared losing his mind. "Nothing but bankruptcy is possible as far as my estate is concerned," Wells wrote. "Do what you can for Mrs. Wells."

Upon his death, the Boston Globe, reported that Wells had once been director of 16 different mining operations, had been a bank president, and "director of many other enterprises." A 1918 history of Colorado said he served on the boards of organizations from Oklahoma to Alaska, and Colorado to California. Another newspaper said Wells had once been worth $10 million to $15 million. But bad investments in Nevada, Idaho, and California had cost him large sums of money. The 1929 stock market crash wiped out what was left.

Several news accounts of Wells' death told of his courage during the Telluride labor wars. Years later, his one-time associate E.B. Adams, lawyer for the Smuggler-Union Company and author of a booklet titled *My Association with a Glamorous Man ... Bulkeley Wells*, also lauded Wells' courage. But, he added, "I suppose that a foolhardy man must be courageous."

Sources: "My Association with a Glamorous Man," by E.B. Adams; "Bulkeley Wells, A.B.," in "History of Colorado," by Wilbur Fisk Stone; "Bulkeley Wells," at www,coloradoencyclopedia.org/article/bulkeley-wells; Colorado historic newspapers at www.coloradohistoricnewspapers.org; other historic newspapers at www.newspapers.com.

CHAPTER 25:
'MANASSA MAULER' HAD LINKS
TO MUCH OF WESTERN COLORADO

In Montrose, Colorado, in the summer of 1912, a 17-year-old fighter who called himself Kid Blackie knocked down his friend and boxing opponent Fred Wood to win one of his earliest sort-of-professional fights. He split the $40 purse with Wood.

Seven years later, Kid Blackie had a different nickname – "The Manassa Mauler" – and a new title: Heavyweight Champion of the World. On the Fourth of July 1919, 24-year-old William Harrison "Jack" Dempsey destroyed the reigning heavyweight champion, giant Jess Willard, in Toledo, Ohio.

Dempsey became known as The Manassa Mauler in part because he was born in the tiny town of Manassa in Colorado's San Luis Valley. But Manassa isn't alone in claiming a connection to Dempsey. Several Colorado communities share in Dempsey's legacy. Montrose played an important role beyond that 1912 fight. The Dempsey family spent several years in Montrose when the Gunnison Tunnel and Uncompahgre Valley Irrigation Project were being built. Dempsey's mother, Celia, operated a restaurant for the tunnel workers until 1909. The future champ helped wash dishes and bus tables.

However, the Dempsey family moved a lot, and records of when and where they lived are not always clear. Author Toby Smith reported they moved to Delta in mid-1907. But Delta County Historical Society records show that Dempsey's father, Hyrum, worked at the Delta Brick and Tile Factory in 1905. Other dates in Dempsey's young life are also disputed.

It is known that Celia and Hyrum Dempsey, originally from West Virginia, arrived in Manassa before the turn of the 20th century, but left the community in 1903 or 1904. They moved first to Creede, Colorado, where Celia worked in a boarding house, then Leadville, Colorado, where she became ill. After a brief stint in Denver, it was back to Colorado's Western Slope, first to Wolcott, then Steamboat Springs, Rifle, and on to a ranch south of Montrose, before finally moving into Montrose proper. Wherever they lived, young Dempsey engaged in amateur pugilism because boxing was a popular activity for poor youngsters. Encouraged by his mother, the boy who was then known as Harry decided he would become a champion one day.

After Montrose, Hyrum moved the Dempsey family to Lakeview, Utah, where Dempsey graduated from elementary school in 1911, just before his

Dempsey 4 – Jack Dempsey, aka Kid Blackie and later, the Manassa Mauler, posing before a fight. Date unknown. *Bain News Service Photograph Collection, Library of Congress.*

16th birthday. Soon afterward he began riding the rails, mostly to towns in Colorado, where he found work as a miner or ranch hand, anything to obtain food. He also boxed. One friend estimated Dempsey fought 450 bouts in the saloons, hotels, and bordellos of Colorado and Utah. Most fights were for meals or a few dollars. Often, he would walk into a saloon and offer to fight any takers for a dollar.

Through these bouts, Dempsey began to develop his boxing skills. He learned to duck and weave, to hit with both fists, to observe his opponents and fight to their weaknesses. He developed a reputation as a tough brawler, although he was a peaceful man outside the ring. He learned from his older brother, Bernie, a not-very-successful professional fighter. Bernie sometimes called himself "Jack" Dempsey, and his younger brother later appropriated that name. The teenage Dempsey also learned pugilistic technique from friends Pat and Andy Malloy in Telluride, where Dempsey worked as a miner. He fought multiple fights there and in Colorado towns from Gunnison to Salida to the Front Range.

He defeated a local champion in Cripple Creek in 1913. He is believed to have fought at the Park Opera House in Grand Junction, but the date and name of his opponent are unknown. A 1915 exhibition in Durango, in which he knocked down his buddy, Andy Malloy, multiple times, is pictured in a mural on the El Rancho Lounge wall in Durango. That same year, Dempsey battered four men at the Grand Junction Hotel and Lunch Counter after he recognized them as thugs who had earlier robbed Dempsey and a Denver newspaper reporter at gunpoint. The reporter described Dempsey as "a destructive dervish" who easily dispatched the four robbers and recovered the stolen money.

In 1916, Dempsey was lured to New York by a fight promoter, but the trip was a disaster. He lost multiple bouts to more experienced boxers and was bilked out of his meager share of purses. In 1917, he fought Pueblo's Fireman Jim Flynn, an experienced heavyweight with a national reputation. Dempsey lost by a technical knockout in the first round, but in a rematch a year later, Dempsey knocked Flynn out in the first round. By then, Dempsey had spent almost a year in Oakland, California, working with manager Jack Kearns. He had a succession of victories over recognized boxers, including seven knockouts in a row. He established a reputation that allowed him to challenge Jess Willard for the heavyweight title in 1919.

The 37-year-old Willard, who was seen by many as indestructible, surrendered to Dempsey after three rounds. Although Dempsey was 50 pounds lighter than Willard and several inches shorter, he "snapped Willard's jaw, pried loose six teeth, broke his cheekbone, squashed his nose, (and) closed one eye," wrote Dempsey biographer Toby Smith. Few boxing fans had ever seen someone punch as hard as Dempsey. Afterward, writer Damon Runyon – who, like

Dempsey, had spent most of his youth in Colorado – dubbed Dempsey "the Manassa Mauler," combining Dempsey's fighting style with his birthplace.

Dempsey held the heavyweight crown for more than seven years. Throughout the 1920s, he and Babe Ruth were the two best known sports figures in the United States. Ruth earned $80,000 a year at his peak, but Dempsey made almost four times that in one fight. His bouts produced the first million-dollar gates in boxing history.

But he also faced scandal. In 1920, Dempsey's ex-wife, a dancehall girl from Utah, accused him of dodging the World War I draft. He was exonerated when it was proved he had legally obtained an exemption as his family's sole breadwinner. Still, the epithet "slacker" dogged him for years.

One of his best-remembered title defenses came in 1923, when he was knocked out of the ring by Argentinian Louis Firpo. He was pushed back by sportswriters, returned to the ring and knocked out Firpo in the second round. However, his most famous fights were two losses to Gene Tunney, first in a ten-round decision in 1926, then in a famous rematch in 1927 with what became known as "the long count." Dempsey knocked Tunney down hard in the seventh round of the 1927 fight, but he didn't retreat to a neutral corner. Tunney lay on the canvas for nearly 15 seconds while the referee waved Dempsey away. Then Tunney got up and won another decision.

Dempsey never regained his title, but he remained a popular ex-champion. Soon after the Tunney fight, he gave up his professional career but continued to stage exhibition fights. Eventually, he opened a restaurant in New York City, where he held court and greeted customers well into the 1970s. Dempsey returned to Colorado several times. He made stops in Denver, and was inducted into Colorado's Sports Hall of Fame in 1965. He went fishing in Gunnison. He traveled to Manassa in the early 1960s to dedicate his boyhood home as a museum.

In 1971, before the start of the first Mohammed Ali-Joe Frasier battle at New York's Madison Square Garden, several former boxing champions were introduced. But Dempsey, seated in the front row, was overlooked by the announcer. The crowd began chanting, "We Want Dempsey! We want Dempsey!" When he was finally introduced and waved to the crowd, the cheers were longer and louder than for any of the others. Nearly 60 years after that Montrose battle, Kid Blackie, better known as Jack Dempsey, remained one of the most popular fighters of all time. That continued until his death at age 87 in New York in 1983.

Sources: "Jack Dempsey," by Jim Wetzel, Delta County Historical Society newsletter, April, 2019; "Kid Blackie: Jack Dempsey's Colorado Days," by Toby Smith; "A Flame of Pure Fire: Jack Dempsey and the Roaring '20s," by Roger Kahn. "Ex-boxing Champion Dempsey Dies at 87," by Shirley Povich, The Washington Post, June 1, 1983 and "Even the Greatest Admired Dempsey," The Atlanta Journal-Constitution, June 2, 1983, at www.newspapers. com.

CHAPTER 26:
AFTER FIVE MARRIAGES, JOSIE MORRIS
CHOSE 50 YEARS OF SOLITUDE

Josie Bassett Morris was 39 years old in 1913 when she acquired a homestead on Cub Creek, an isolated canyon 10 miles from Jensen, Utah. She would live there another 50 years. By the time she moved to Cub Creek, Josie had already been a cowgirl and a mother of two sons. She had operated three boarding houses. She may have had a youthful romance with Butch Cassidy. She had been married five times, and she had been accused of killing one of her husbands.

But then, Josie was known as the more demure of the two Bassett sisters.

Josie and Ann Bassett were raised in rough-and-tumble Brown's Park in Northwestern Colorado, along with three brothers. They knew Indians and outlaws growing up, learned to ride and punch cattle. The same year that Josie moved onto the Cub Creek ranch, Ann Bassett was found not guilty in a famous cattle theft trial in Craig, Colorado, where she had already been dubbed "the Queen of the Cattle Rustlers."

Josie Morris, né Bassett, settled down to a pleasant life on her isolated Utah ranch, although her life was not what most people – even mountain dwellers in the early 20th century – would call routine. She made corn whiskey and apricot brandy and sold the alcohol during Prohibition. She was indicted for cattle rustling but was not convicted. She killed deer as needed, with little worry for hunting licenses or seasons.

Although she lived alone much of the time, Josie was no hermit. Her son Crawford, his wife and children lived with her a few years before moving to Vernal, Utah. Even then, the children spent summers at the Cub Creek ranch. Josie's sister Ann and her husband were frequent visitors, as was her father, Herb Bassett. Nearby ranchers or people on their way from Brown's Park to Vernal stopped for dinner or coffee. Josie raised cattle, hogs, sheep, and chickens. She had a marvelous garden and shared her bounty with everyone: her son's family, cabin visitors and poor people living in Jensen and Vernal.

Unlike Sister Anne, Josie Bassett was not a native of Colorado. She was born in Arkansas in 1874, before the family made the move west in 1877 and settled in Brown's Park. Once there, Herb Bassett was a rancher, but he also spent time as postmaster, justice of the peace and county commissioner. Much of the day-to-day ranch oversight was left to his wife, Elizabeth, who rode

Josie 2 – Josie Bassett Morris at the stove in her cabin at farm on Cub Creek, North-eastern Utah. Date unknown. *Used by permission, Uintah County Library Regional History Center, all rights reserved.*

horseback over rough country, gathered cattle, was well-educated and served as a role model for her two daughters.

It was rumored that Josie had a brief romance with Robert LeRoy Parker, who later became known as Butch Cassidy, when she was a teenager. Ann Bassett was infatuated with Butch's friend, Elzy Lay. Neither woman ever confirmed these romantic rumors, but they admitted knowing and befriending the men.

Soon, however, Josie was in a much more serious relationship. On March 21, 1893 – when she was 19 – she married Jim McKnight, a cowboy in the Bassett bunkhouse. Their son, Crawford, was born four months later. A second son known as Chick was born in 1896. The couple established a ranch about 10 miles from the Bassett ranch, and Josie was happy with her life.

Jim, however, wanted to move to Vernal and start a saloon. Josie refused, so Jim left her. Josie filed for divorce in March 1900, and Jim McKnight was shot in April by a deputy trying to serve divorce papers. McKnight recovered, however. He opened his saloon and started a horse ranch near Vernal. Josie sold the ranch she and McKnight had developed in Brown's Park and moved to Craig, Colorado, where she operated a boarding house. It was there she met her second husband, druggist Charles Raney, a man seven years' Josie's senior. They married in April 1902 and Josie quit the boarding-house business.

However, Josie's sons hated Raney's strict discipline, and by 1906, Josie had had enough of him as well. She left one day, moved to Baggs, Wyoming, and started another boarding house. In July 1906, she was married for the third time, to a former railroad worker and prize-fighter named Charles Williams. He left in November, apparently eager for life in a larger city. Josie filed for divorce two years later. She and the boys moved to Rock Springs, Wyoming, where she again ran a boarding house and her sons completed high school.

In 1911, Josie moved back to Brown's Park and rented a ranch with her fourth husband, Emerson Wells. Those who knew Wells said he was a good rancher and a nice guy, except when he was on one of his frequent alcoholic binges. On New Year's Eve 1912, the couple attended a dance in Linwood, Utah. Wells got plastered for several days and nights. By the morning of January 2, he was feeling terrible. Josie gave him coffee and tried to soothe him. But he writhed in pain and then, she said, "he just straightened right back and died." Josie discussed the death with the local constable, but no autopsy was held and no death certificate signed. The next day, Josie took Wells' body to Brown's Park for burial.

Later, a longtime friend of the Bassett family named Minnie Crouse, who owned the hotel where Josie and Emerson stayed for the New Year's Eve gathering, claimed she heard the couple arguing loudly. She also said she had discovered strychnine among Josie's things at the hotel. She was convinced Josie had poisoned Wells, and she freely shared her beliefs. Others soon accepted the story. But strychnine was often found in patent medicines advertised for curing alcoholism. Some people believed if Josie had poisoned her fourth husband, it was accidentally as she tried to get him to quit drinking. In any event, the sheriff questioned Josie, but no inquest was held and no charges were filed.

Josie returned to the leased ranch in Brown's Park, which she operated with the help of a cowhand named Ben Morris. When her lease ran out, she moved to Utah, and Ben moved with her. They were married on November 24, 1913. Josie staked her claim to 160 acres at Cub Creek that same winter, and the couple moved into a tent on the property the next spring. After living with the foul-mouthed Morris for two years, Josie had had enough. She gave Morris 15 minutes to clear out. He was gone in five. That was the end of Josie's marriages, although exactly when she and Morris were divorced is unclear. She later reportedly became involved with, but never married, a neighbor named Ed Lewis.

An ongoing dispute with a different neighbor led to her indictment for cattle rustling in 1936. She abandoned the overalls she normally wore and appeared at trial in her best little-old-lady dress. Two trials resulted in two hung juries, and the prosecution gave up.

When Josie was 90, she slipped on the ice while feeding her horse and broke her hip. She crawled into her cabin and sat alone, without food, water or a fire for two days until her son found her. She was taken to a hospital in Salt Lake, and died there in May, 1964.

In 1915, a major paleontological site 10 miles from her home became Dinosaur National Monument. It has expanded since then, and eventually acquired the site of Josie Bassett Morris' homestead. The National Park Service manages the site for visitors today.

Sources: "The Bassett Women," by Grace McClure; "Queen Ann of Brown's Park," by Ann Bassett Willis, Colorado Magazine, April 1952; "Nighthawk Rising," by Diana Allen Kouris; Josie Bassett Morris homestead, Dinosaur National Monument.

PART SIX:
CRIME AND JUSTICE

Great Train Rob – A lithograph for a theatrical production called the Great Train Robbery, circa 1896. *Strobidge Lith. Co., Library of Congress.*

CHAPTER 27:
'BLOODHOUND' DOC SHORES WAS
RELENTLESS PURSUING TRAIN ROBBERS

When four men robbed a Denver & Rio Grande Railroad train near Grand Junction, Colorado, on November 3, 1887, Mesa County Sheriff J.O. Bradish formed a posse. Two days later, the posse disbanded, frustrated by the inability to find a trace of the outlaws. The same day the posse abandoned its search, Gunnison County Sheriff Cyrus "Doc" Shores showed up at the robbery site. He did not give up.

Over the next three months, Shores, who was also a deputy U.S. marshal, traveled nearly 600 miles on foot and horseback pursuing the bandits. He also journeyed at least 5,000 miles by train, riding repeatedly across Colorado, Kansas, and part of Utah. By early February, 1888, Shores and his men had arrested all four outlaws.

Cyrus Wells Shores was born in 1844 near Detroit, Michigan. He acquired the nickname "Doc" after caring for an orphan lamb when he was five years old. Moving west as a teenager, Shores worked as a hunter, freighter and cattle drover. He arrived in Gunnison, Colorado, in May 1880. In autumn 1883, Shores was elected Gunnison County Sheriff. Later in his life he became a railroad investigator, then chief of police in Salt Lake City. But he was still in Gunnison when he received word of the 1887 holdup near Grand Junction, which a Salida, Colorado, newspaper called the first train robbery in the state. Shores received a telegram from the U.S. marshal in Denver, "asking me to do everything possible to help apprehend the culprits."

The train robbery occurred in an isolated canyon between the tiny community of Whitewater, Colorado, and Grand Junction. The outlaws piled rocks and timbers on the railroad tracks five miles southeast of Grand Junction at a spot called Unaweep Switch along the Gunnison River. When the train halted, the robbers climbed into the baggage car and demanded the clerk open the safe. But the clerk said only a station agent could open it and the outlaws gave up on the safe. Shores said later the safe contained "several thousand dollars." Another account said it held $75,000. The bandits total take in the robbery "did not exceed $150," Shores said. Even so, a $4,000 reward was offered, a significant inducement to a poor sheriff, Shores acknowledged.

The bandits were later determined to be Ed Rhodes, Bob Boyd, and brothers Bob and Jack (or Jim) Smith. Bob Smith had worked on a ranch in Un-

Doc Shores – Cyrus Wells "Doc" Shores as he appeared later in life. Date unknown. *Image courtesy of the Museums of Western Colorado.*

aweep Canyon, and his brother may have briefly been the D&RG station agent in Whitewater.

The afternoon of November 4, the day after the robbery, Shores caught the train from Gunnison to Grand Junction, 125 miles away. He was accompanied by his brother-in-law, M.L. Allison. At 2 a.m. November 5, they arrived at Unaweep Switch. At dawn, they began searching for signs of the bandits on the north side of the Gunnison River. They gave up at dusk and caught the train into Grand Junction. The next day, Shores and Allison "rented two broken-down saddle horses" and searched the south side of the Gunnison River. They found the tracks of four men on foot, and in two days, trailed them 20 miles up Bangs Canyon, south of Grand Junction, before losing the trail.

Over the next few months Shores continued his search by multiple means. Unimpressed with the horses available in Grand Junction, he took the train back to Gunnison to get three of his own horses, which he then shipped to Grand Junction. Shores, Allison, and D&RG investigator Jim Duckworth rode those horses through the length of Unaweep Canyon, more than 50 miles southwest of Grand Junction.

Near today's community of Gateway, Colorado, rancher Tom Denning led Shores and his colleagues to Sinbad Valley, where four men afoot had been spotted. The lawmen spent a night outdoors in a rainstorm, then hunkered down in a dugout cabin for three days as the rain turned to snow. Snow obliterated the outlaws' trail, so Shores, Allison and Duckworth opted to return to Grand Junction. But the snow was too deep in Unaweep, so they headed south, first to the Paradox Valley, then to the mining town of Placerville. They finally arrived back in Grand Junction days later. Duckworth, who had contracted pneumonia during the miserable weather, died soon thereafter.

If Shores mourned for his colleague, he did not let it slow him down. He soon embarked on a 365-mile train trip through Delta and Gunnison, Colorado, over Marshal Pass, then to Cañon City, and Denver. (The railroad did not yet run directly east from Grand Junction, so he had to take this roundabout route.) In Denver, he met with officials of the D&RG and the Pinkerton National Detective Agency. Then, with fresh instructions and evidence, he headed back over the same rail route to Grand Junction.

Once there, he received word that the outlaws had been spotted at Ravensbeque, about 20 miles east of Grand Junction near present-day De Beque, Colorado. It was a false alarm, but it led Shores and Allison on a 100-mile round-trip horseback trek. (There were other false sightings, placing the outlaws on Grand Mesa and in Vernal, Utah. Shores did not follow them.)

In Grand Junction once more, they discovered the outlaws had stashed a homemade boat in the brush near town, then had left in it. Pieces of an old almanac and red wool found in Bangs Canyon matched those found at the boat site. Shores followed the men on horseback. He rode some 60 miles along the river to Cisco, Utah, where he learned that four men had recently arrived by boat, having somehow managed to navigate through or around Westwater rapids. Shores continued to Green River, Utah, where he learned the four men had gone to Price, Utah.

Before he could continue, he received a telegram from the Pinkerton Agency urging him to go to Denver immediately. So it was back on the Denver & Rio Grande route through Delta, Montrose, Gunnison and over Marshal Pass to Denver. There, he met Pinkerton Agent Charlie Siringo. Shores and Siringo embarked on another wild-goose chase – 385 miles one way by train to Cawker City, Kansas, where the Smith brothers were said to be hiding. They were not.

Meanwhile, Shores sent Allison, Mesa County Sheriff Brandish and Shores's undersheriff to apprehend the outlaws in Price. They captured three men, and Shores met them in Thompson Springs, Utah, on their way to Denver. Shores learned that the fourth man, known as Bob Wallace, who might have been Bob Boyd, lived near Paola, Kansas. So, in mid-January 1888, he headed to Paola, a round-trip train journey of 1,300 miles from Denver. He determined the man was Boyd, but by then he was working in Price, Utah. Shores returned to Denver, then headed back to Utah.

"Between trains in Gunnison, I went home to see my family for a moment," he wrote in his memoirs.

Near Price, Utah, he arrested Boyd and held off a half-dozen of Boyd's mining coworkers who threatened to break the prisoner free. Shores took Boyd to Denver, where all four outlaws faced trial on federal charges. They were found guilty and sent to the federal penitentiary at Laramie, Wyoming.

After his capture, Ed Rhodes told Shores, "You're the damnedest bloodhound I ever seen."

Sources: "Memoirs of a Lawman," by Doc Shores, edited by Wilson Rockwell; the Museums of Western Colorado; Colorado historic newspapers at www.coloradohistoricnewspapers.org and Utah historic newspapers at www.digitalnewspapers.org.

CHAPTER 28:
CASTLE GATE ROBBERY PUT
BUTCH CASSIDY AMONG OUTLAW ELITE

———

When the Pleasant Valley Coal Company in Castle Gate, Utah, was robbed of more than $7,000 in payroll on April 21, 1897, it was called the boldest theft in Utah history. With good reason. Two men pulled off the heist in broad daylight while more than 100 people stood nearby. The two bandits then raced down the canyon on speedy horses toward Price, Utah and galloped into infamy.

Butch Cassidy was soon named as one of the robbers, identified by mine paymaster E. L. Carpenter, who had looked directly at the outlaw over the barrel of Cassidy's gun. Cassidy had confronted Carpenter and another mine employee at the base of the stairs leading to their second-floor office as they carried the payroll in bags with silver and gold. Cassidy snatched a bag of gold from Carpenter, and picked up a bag of silver that the other man had dropped when Cassidy hit him with his pistol. With the aid of his companion, Elzy Lay, Cassidy mounted his skittish horse. The pair then galloped down the canyon, and were out of range before the shocked bystanders grabbed guns and began shooting.

Cassidy dropped the heavy bag of silver, but kept the gold. With relays of fresh horses, he and Lay outran pursuers. By an arduous route, they made it to Green River, then to the outlaw hideout known as Robber's Roost, east of Hanksville, Utah.

The brazen crime had been meticulously planned. Swift horses were taught to handle the noise and commotion. Associates provided fresh horses at important locations along the escape route that ran past Price. There was even a northern escape plan, in case the southern route was blocked. The outlaws looked even more ingenious when two posses chasing them that day shot at each other before they figured out they were on the same side.

The boldness of the payroll theft cemented Cassidy's growing notoriety.

"One of the most daring robberies that ever took place in the West," said the *Ogden Daily Standard* the day after the robbery.

Castle Gate "did more to make Butch Cassidy famous in outlaw circles than any other single exploit," wrote author Charles Kelly in 1959.

When Butch, Elzy and their colleagues celebrated in Baggs, Wyoming, that July, galloping and firing their pistols, shooting holes in a saloon, then paying

Butch Prison – Robert LeRoy Parker, alias Butch Cassidy, in photo taken while he was incarcerated in the Wyoming State Prison. *The Library of Congress.*

the bar owner for every bullet hole, their reputation only grew.

Cassidy was born Robert LeRoy Parker in Beaver, Utah, in 1866. He spent his youth around Circleville, Utah, and became expert at breaking horses and wrangling cattle. He probably also engaged in some horse and cattle rustling then.

William Ellsworth "Elzy" Lay was born in Ohio in 1869, but he was raised in Northeastern Colorado. He met Cassidy in the late 1880s, and the two hung out together in Brown's Park in Northwestern Colorado.

Cassidy graduated to major crime in August, 1889, when he joined Matt Warner and Tom McCarty to rob the San Miguel Valley Bank in Telluride. McCarty, the older of the three, planned the successful holdup and taught Butch the importance of having multiple escape routes and friends waiting with relays of fresh horses.

After Telluride, Cassidy limited his criminal activity to livestock theft. It was the alleged stealing of horses – animals Cassidy claimed he had purchased legitimately – that landed him in the Wyoming State Prison in 1894. He was pardoned in January 1896 after promising he would commit no more crimes in Wyoming. Then Butch learned that Matt Warner was facing trial for murder.

By then, Warner was married and attempting to go straight. He was hired to protect mining claims near Vernal, Utah. But when he and another man confronted would-be claim jumpers, a gun battle ensued. Two of the claim jumpers were killed and the third injured. Warner and his companion were arrested for murder.

Cassidy first offered to break Warner out of jail. But at Warner's request, he decided to raise money for Warner's defense – by robbing a bank. On August 13, 1896 – seven months after his release from prison – Butch, with Elzy and a third man called Bob Meeks, robbed the bank at Montpelier, Idaho, just across the border from Wyoming. They made off with $7,165, and used relays of fresh horses to evade pursuers.

The Montpelier robbery was big news in the West, but it didn't garner the same notoriety for Butch Cassidy that the Castle Gate robbery did eight months later. Neither he nor Lay was named as a suspect until a month afterward.

Following the Montpelier heist, Butch and Elzy spent much of the winter of 1896-1897 in Robber's Roost, with Elzy's wife Maude and a second woman. While there, they also planned the Castle Gate job. They "knew it would require careful planning down to the smallest detail, so they took nearly a year in planning," wrote Butch's great-great nephew, Bill Betensen. "They trained horses for their escape during their stay at Robber's Roost."

In March, Butch was working on ranches in the Huntington, Utah, area south of Price. Butch and Elzy began visiting Price and Castle Gate, running their horses up and down the canyon, telling people they were training them for upcoming horse races. They wanted to be familiar faces in the small mining community before the theft.

Butch was drinking in a Castle Gate saloon when the train pulled in with the payroll aboard. He and Elzy had arranged to have their confederates cut telegraph lines, so news of the crime would be delayed in reaching other communities.

Immediately after the robbery, E.L. Carpenter commandeered a train engine at Castle Gate, and with a few well-armed men, steamed down the tracks toward Price in pursuit of the outlaws. But Butch and Elzy hid behind a section house as the train passed. Then it was on to Robber's Roost. The search for the Castle Gate bandits was abandoned by May 6, 1897, because lawmen then viewed Robber's Roost as a nearly impenetrable outlaw fortress.

A year after Castle Gate, newspapers around the country ran articles that described Cassidy as the leader of a massive gang of "bloodthirsty" outlaws, whose actions had provoked governors of Western states to confer on how to exterminate the gang.

The first claim was a wild exaggeration. The Wild Bunch, led by Cassidy, never had more than two dozen loosely affiliated members. But the second report was accurate. In 1898, the governors of Utah, Wyoming and Colorado hatched a plan to capture or eliminate outlaws who hid out in Robber's Roost, the Hole in the Wall in Wyoming and Brown's Park in Colorado.

In May 1898 came the startling news that Butch Cassidy had been killed by lawmen near Thompson Springs, Utah, along with another outlaw named Joe Walker. Two others were captured. The reports were false. When a Wyoming sheriff who knew Butch examined the body, he declared it wasn't Cassidy's. Butch took the news with good humor. Through an acquaintance he complimented Utah Governor Heber M. Wells "for his good judgment in refusing to pay the state reward for his [Butch's] apprehension," the *Salt Lake Tribune* reported.

State authorities and newspaper editors may have wanted Butch Cassidy captured or even dead. But few people in rural Utah did. "The leader of the Wild Bunch was a friendly, gay, reckless, and coolly daring young man whom everyone liked, even the sheriffs who chased him," wrote Utah author Wallace Stegner in the 1940s.

Cassidy is known to have participated in no more than a half-dozen major thefts in the West, and he probably helped plan others. By early 1901, he and Harry Longabaugh, aka the Sundance Kid, were on their way to South America with Longabaugh's girlfriend Ethel Place. There, they ranched, committed more crimes, and may or may not have been killed in a shootout with Bolivian authorities. The Cassidy mystique continued to grow.

Meanwhile, Elzy Lay was imprisoned in New Mexico after taking part in a train robbery and subsequent shootout in which a sheriff was killed. Lay was released from prison in 1905 and went straight. He died in California in 1934.

Aided by an attorney hired by Butch Cassidy, Matt Warner was convicted of manslaughter instead of murder. He served just over three years in prison before he was pardoned. He later became a town marshal in Price.

In 1901, the Pleasant Valley Coal Company suffered a worse disaster than the payroll robbery, when an explosion at its mine near Castle Gate killed 200 miners.

Sources: "Butch Cassidy, My Uncle," by Bill Betenson; "The Outlaw Trail: The Story of Butch Cassidy," by Charles Kelly; "The Castle Gate Payroll Robbery," by Joel Frandsen, WOLA Journal, Winter, 2007; "Mormon Country," by Wallace Stegner; "The Wild Bunch: Wild, but not much of a bunch," Daniel Buck and Anne Meadows, True West Magazine, November-December 2002; "Explosion of Pleasant Valley Coal Company," by Ronald G. Watt, Utah History to Go, May 3, 2016; Historic newspapers at www.newspapers.com and https://newspapers.lib.utah.edu.

CHAPTER 29:
RANGE WAR PROVOKED GUNFIGHT,
KILLINGS IN ESCALANTE CANYON

As Cash Sampson and Ben Lowe rode side-by-side through Escalante Canyon near Delta, Colorado, on June 9, 1917, they argued vehemently. In a few moments, they drew guns and blew each other from their saddles. They died within 50 feet of each other.

Sampson and Lowe were not friends. There was considerable enmity between them. Each had a ranch nearby, and on the day they died, they had eaten lunch together at the cabin of fellow rancher J.W. Musser. Musser later said the luncheon was tense, but no harsh words were spoken.

No one saw the shooting, but two people were within hearing – Ben Lowe's two young sons who had been riding with their father. The Lowes left the Musser cabin about 15 minutes ahead of Sampson, but he caught up with them. Ben Lowe told his sons to ride ahead, which they did, but they galloped back at the sound of gunfire to find their father dying and Sampson already dead.

Did the killings occur because Sampson accused Lowe of cattle rustling, as newspaper accounts of the time suggested? Did it involve horse theft, as one report said? Or did it involve Sampson's investigation of a year-old sheep slaughter by area cattlemen and Lowe's probable involvement in that slaughter?

Sampson, then 46, was a former Delta County Sheriff who had also served as a Colorado brand inspector and a deputy U.S. marshal. He resigned his job as sheriff in 1914 to resume his brand-inspector duties. In 1916, not long after the sheep killings, he bought a ranch on Escalante Creek. Sampson was a bachelor, well-liked in Delta County and respected by area cattlemen, according to contemporary reports.

Ben Lowe was nearing his 50th birthday when he died. He was married and had three daughters and two sons. Lowe had a reputation as an excellent horseman and cattleman. He had a fierce temper, but he maintained equally fierce loyalty to those he trusted. At one time, he was known for his heavy drinking and carousing, but that had apparently stopped several years earlier, when he moved his family from a ranch west of Delta to one in Escalante Canyon.

The deaths of Sampson and Lowe occurred in Mesa County, Colorado, near where Delta, Mesa, and Montrose counties meet in Escalante Canyon, about 20 miles south of today's U.S. Highway 50. Based on gun cartridges at the scene and the way the two bodies were sprawled, a coroner's inquest concluded

Ben Lowe and kids – Rancher Ben Lowe and his two sons, not long before he was killed in a shootout in Escalante Canyon. *Courtesy of Delta County Historical Society.*

that Lowe fired three shots from his revolver, while Sampson shot only once with his pistol.

According to a *Montrose Daily Press* article at the time, the inquest determined, "The men rode side by side for a short distance, quarreling. Then Lowe pulled his gun and fired at Sampson, missing him." Sampson reached for his gun and shot once, striking Lowe in the back as Lowe leaned far over his saddle "to get behind his horse." Sampson's bullet pierced Lowe's heart and lungs and knocked him from his horse. But, as Lowe lay on the ground, he fired twice more. The first of these shots struck Sampson in the head, blew away a large part of his skull. After Sampson hit the ground, with one foot stuck in his stirrup, Lowe fired his third shot, this time striking Sampson in the thigh.

Lowe's two sons, Robert, age 11, and William, 9, returned just in time to hear their father call for them. But he apparently died as they reached his side, without saying anything more. One or both boys raced back to the Musser ranch for help. Musser and his hired hand galloped to the scene and found the bodies.

Lowe had run-ins with the law as early as 1904, but they had not involved Sampson. Later, as a brand inspector, Sampson became convinced Lowe was involved in cattle rustling in the area. A *Grand Junction Daily Sentinel* article published on June 11, 1917, said Sampson accused Lowe of cattle rustling on multiple occasions, but no convictions were reported. The *Sentinel* story mentioned another potential reason for the fight: An Escalante Creek rancher accused Lowe of stealing a colt a few days before the shootings, and Sampson confirmed that Lowe had branded over the other man's brand. Also on June 11, the *Montrose Daily Press* report said, "The same two men had a bitter quarrel in the streets of Delta a few years ago."

Nearly 50 years after the killings, in his 1965 book *Uncompahgre Country*, author Wilson Rockwell suggested the range war was the reason for the quarrel and killings. Lowe had been among a group of cattlemen who killed hundreds of sheep near Escalante Canyon in 1916 to discourage sheepmen from moving onto the cattle range, Rockwell said. A year later, Sampson was investigating the sheep killings.

"Within the near future Cash [Sampson] was to testify against Ben [Lowe] at a grand jury investigation concerning a cattle-sheep fight ..." Rockwell wrote. "Consequently, it is quite possible that this pending grand jury investigation was the delicate topic of their heated conversation."

In 1972, Carl M. Gilbert wrote a lengthy article about the Delta County sheep war for *The Daily Sentinel's* Sunday magazine. Gilbert was a teenage cowboy on his father's ranch in Escalante Canyon when the cattlemen killed sheep in 1916. Gilbert participated in the sheep slaughter, as did Ben Lowe and several other ranchers, he said. By 1917, Gilbert was working on a ranch in Utah. He was not around when Sampson and Lowe killed each other. Still, he heard of it from his family and other ranchers. Gilbert noted that Sampson had moved onto an Escalante Canyon ranch less than a year before the double killing. He suggested cattlemen, including Lowe, "were suspicious that he had been sent by the sheepmen to spy, to get evidence about the sheep killings."

Another man with ties to both victims, J.D. Dillard, wrote a letter published by the *Sentinel* in 1973, which supported the range-war theory. Dillard was Cash Sampson's nephew, and he married one of Lowe's daughters years after the shooting. Dillard said he believed Sampson planned to arrest Lowe over the sheep killings, even though his sympathy was with the cattlemen. "I know this disturbed Uncle Cash greatly because I heard him discussing it with Mother," Dillard wrote. But Sampson was acting on orders from then-Mesa County District Attorney William Weisner, who had empaneled a grand jury to investigate the sheep killings, Dillard said.

In any event, the two men argued that day as they rode side-by-side in the canyon, then shot and killed each other in one of the most unusual double murders in Western Colorado history. More than a century later, it is impossible to know what was said between the two men that provoked gunfire. But their deaths likely were a consequence of the ongoing fight between cattle ranchers and sheepmen that raged off and on for decades.

Sources: Historic editions of the Montrose Daily Press and Delta County Independent at www.coloradohistoricnewspapers.org; Historic editions of The Daily Sentinel at www. newspapers.com; "Uncompahgre Country," by Wilson Rockwell; the Museums of Western Colorado and Delta County Historical Society.

CHAPTER 30:
DEPUTY'S MURDER SPARKED OUTRAGE
AND QUICK JUSTICE IN 1906

Edward Innes was a well-liked young man and the beloved son of the first elected sheriff of Mesa County, Colorado. He had been a respected fire chief in the city of Grand Junction, Colorado. By 1906, he was a deputy in the Mesa County Jail, noted for treating inmates kindly. When he was murdered by one of those inmates on September 26, 1906, the community was outraged and justice was swift.

- The accused killer, John "George" McGarvey, was captured on September 30, 1906, after a furious manhunt.
- McGarvey's trial began on October 3 and concluded the next day with a guilty verdict.
- He was sentenced to death on October 5.
- He was hanged on January 12, 1907.

The man McGarvey killed, Edward Innes, was born in 1878 on Colorado's Front Range. But he was raised in Mesa County and graduated from Grand Junction High School. His father, William Innes, operated a sawmill near Whitewater, Colorado when he moved his family to the Western Slope in 1882. William Innes served two non-consecutive terms as sheriff, the first beginning in 1883, shortly after Mesa County was established. He was elected again in 1892 and served through 1896.

His son Edward became Grand Junction's fire chief about 1901. When he was reappointed by the Grand Junction City Council in 1903, the *Grand Junction Daily Sentinel* reported, "His record has been so good that there was no contesting nominee and his election for this important position was made by acclamation."

He ran a professional department and helped to modernize its equipment. He was also in charge of Curley, "the little dog at the fire station" who "is always to be found at the heels of Chief Innes when there is a fire," the *Sentinel* said.

Despite this record, and even though volunteer firefighters petitioned to have him retained, the City Council declined to reappoint Innes as fire chief in 1905. So, Innes went to work for then-Mesa County Sheriff William Struthers as a deputy in the county jail. Innes was single and lived with his parents at their home at 755 Ouray Ave. But he was no shrinking violet, according to the

Sentinel: "No young man in Grand Junction was held in higher regard or had more friends than Edward Innes."

The Mesa County Fair was underway the last week of September 1906. Consequently, Sheriff Struthers and most of his deputies were not near the jail on the evening Innes was attacked. Innes was the only officer at the jail about 5 p.m., watching several inmates play cards. McGarvey was in the corridor with Innes, as was a 16-year-old youngster named Charles Van Horn, who had stolen a bicycle. McGarvey had been in jail since April, accused of raping a 12-year-old girl. But he appeared sickly, and Innes "was inclined to allow the man some privileges as a trusty," the *Sentinel* reported the day after the attack. "For this privilege and kindness the brute has shown his gratitude by attempting to kill the man who befriended him," the paper added, going to print before Innes perished from his wounds.

On the evening of the attack, McGarvey grabbed a heavy piece of kindling wood, snuck up behind Innes and smashed him in the head, proclaiming "I got you this time, Eddie!" Van Horn, cowering in a corner, was the only eyewitness. The card-playing inmates only saw McGarvey after he grabbed Innes' revolver and threatened to kill any prisoner who made noise. When McGarvey disappeared into the falling dusk, the inmates yelled to pedestrians outside. One pedestrian found Sheriff Struthers, and he soon arrived with deputies and doctors.

There were reports of a furtive-looking man heading south toward the Colorado River, and a tracking dog followed a scent to a sugar-beet plant near the river. Telephone calls were made throughout the county, telling people to be on the lookout for a late-20s, clean-shaven man with black hair, about 5-feet, 4-inches tall, weighing around 130 pounds. Searchers had no success the first few days, and a reward for McGarvey's capture grew from $50 to $500.

Late on September 29, two days after Innes had died from his injuries, a man thought to be McGarvey was spotted near a swamp along the Colorado River, six miles east of Grand Junction. Carrying torches and weapons, 150 men surrounded the swamp and waited until dawn. But they found no fugitive. The sighting was an error. McGarvey had not gone that way. Instead, he headed northeast to Palisade. There, he jumped a train but rode just a few miles before a conductor threw him off near the coal-mining town of Cameo. He struck out on foot.

Early on September 30, McGarvey appeared at William McDowell's ranch, two miles west of De Beque, Colorado, looking ragged and begging for food. McDowell suspected this was the wanted man, and he offered him temporary work cutting firewood. Once McGarvey was busy working, McDowell got his shotgun, aimed it at the fugitive and demanded his surrender. He also retrieved the pistol McGarvey had taken from Innes. He took McGarvey into De Beque,

Deputy Innes – Mesa County Sheriff's Deputy Edward Innes, far right, who was killed by an inmate in 1906. This photo shows him when he was with the Grand Junction, Colorado Fire Department, along with Firemen John Dickerson (seated) and Del Newell, along with the firehouse dog, Curly. *Image courtesy of the Museums of Western Colorado.*

where he was held until Sheriff Struthers arrived. Struthers and his undersheriff immediately took the prisoner east by train. Although there was no hint of mob violence, "The officers, wanting to be on the safe side, thought it best to take McGarvey to Glenwood Springs until the day of the trial," the *Sentinel* reported.

The trial occurred on October 3 and continued the next day. Van Horn testified, as did several other inmates. So did Sheriff Struthers, his undersheriff, and the county coroner. McGarvey's court-appointed attorney did not dispute the testimony. He argued that the killing was not premeditated and that McGarvey only wanted to incapacitate Innes.

The defense arguments failed to move the jurors. At 4 p.m. October 4, the jury found McGarvey guilty of first-degree murder. On October 5, Judge Theron Stevens ordered McGarvey hanged at the penitentiary in Cañon City the following January. The judge also told McGarvey, "You should be wiped from the face of the earth ... Had you one hundred lives, the taking of them all could not atone for the foul crime."

After his trial, McGarvey worked unsuccessfully to get a new trial or to have his sentence commuted. He also pleaded for help from his father in New Jersey, Bernard McGarvey, a well-to-do property owner. The elder McGarvey was appalled by the rape charge and then the murder of Innes, and he wanted nothing to do with his son. After Bernard's mother – John McGarvey's grandmother – implored him to act, Bernard McGarvey finally did so. He sent letters to Colorado Governor Henry Buchtel, pleading for mercy for his son. He was too late. The letters reached the governor just days after the sentence was carried out and John McGarvey was hanged.

Few people in Mesa County shed any tears for McGarvey. In fact, the *Sentinel* reported on January 24, 1907, that there was a new display in the Grand Junction Fire Department: In a glass case on the fire house wall was the noose that hanged McGarvey.

Edward Innes, the first Mesa County law enforcement officer to die in the line of duty, was added to the Colorado Law Enforcement Officers' Memorial in 2000. In 2007, his name was added to the National Law Enforcement Officers' Memorial in Washington, D.C. No other employee of the Mesa County Sheriff's Office died in the line of duty for more than 100 years, until Deputy Derek Geer was shot and killed on February 8, 2016.

Sources: Historic editions of The Daily Sentinel online at www.newspapers.com; Mesa County Sheriff's Office Wall of Honor.

CHAPTER 31:
PINKERTON MAN ON BANDITS' TRAIL
WAS FREQUENTLY IN MESA COUNTY

When Pinkerton National Detective Agency operative Charlie Siringo began his four-year odyssey to track down the men who robbed a train in Tipton, Wyoming, he started in Grand Junction, Colorado. By the time he closed his investigation in 1904, he had "traveled more than 25,000 miles by rail, vehicles, afoot and on horseback." Siringo made no arrests during the lengthy effort, but he still considered it a success. "During these four years of strenuous life ... I secured much valuable information for the Dickenson agency," he wrote.

That's no misprint. "Dickenson" meant "Pinkerton" in Siringo's book, *A Cowboy Detective, A True Story of Twenty-two Years with a World Famous Detective Agency*. Siringo retired from the Pinkertons in 1907 and began writing about his detective career. But his former boss, William Pinkerton, was not happy with Siringo's book. After a legal battle, Siringo was forced to use fictitious names in many instances. The Pinkerton agency became the Dickenson agency. Siringo's immediate supervisor and mentor, James McParland, became "James McCartney." Notorious killer and one-time Pinkerton agent Tom Horn became "Tim Corn." Siringo used the correct – but often misspelled – names for outlaws such as Butch Cassidy, Harry Longabaugh, known as the Sundance Kid, and Harvey Logan, aka Kid Curry.

Charles Angelo Siringo was born on the Texas Gulf Coast in 1855, and grew up when wild cattle grazed over much of Texas. While still in his teens, Siringo became a cowboy, first in Southern Texas, then in the West Texas badlands. He eventually joined cattle drives from Texas to the new railroad shipping centers in Kansas. In 1885, he published his first book, *A Texas Cowboy, or Fifteen Years on the Hurricane Deck of a Spanish Pony*. Considered the first cowboy autobiography, it appeared as Americans were becoming enthralled with cowboy life. His book did not make him rich, but it provided some money for the budding author. He moved to Chicago with his wife and young daughter in 1886, planning to become a writer.

However, within months of his move, the Haymarket Square Riot occurred in Chicago when a bomb exploded during a labor demonstration. In its aftermath, the Pinkerton Agency, headquartered in Chicago, actively recruited new agents. Siringo joined and was assigned to Pinkerton's Denver office. His family moved to Colorado with him. Working undercover, Siringo helped solve

Charles A. Siringo – Pinkerton Detective Charles A. Siringo, circa 1900. *Public Domain Photo, Wikimedia Commons.*

a political dispute in Southern Colorado. Next, he partnered with Gunnison County Sheriff Cyrus "Doc" Shores to track down four train robbers. By the time of the Tipton, Wyoming, train robbery on August 29, 1900, Siringo had successfully solved a Nevada mine theft, helped foil political insurrection in New Mexico, and barely escaped alive while investigating an Idaho mine strike.

After some time off, he arrived back in Denver in early September 1900 and was immediately sent to Grand Junction, Colorado. "Our agency had just received a 'tip' through an ex-convict in Grand Junction," that two of the Tipton bandits were camped on a mesa 20 miles from the town, Siringo wrote. "Therefore, I was hustled right out to get on the trail of these two men."

Several posses had chased the Tipton robbers in Wyoming after the train holdup. However, *The Daily Sentinel* in Grand Junction reported on September 5, 1900, that the official search had been abandoned because the trail was cold. The thieves "gained so much time on the officers that capture seems out of the question," the paper said.

But Pinkerton agents weren't so easily deterred. Siringo acquired two horses and supplies, then set out through Unaweep Canyon southeast of Grand Junction, after learning that the thieves had visited notorious cattle rustler Lafe Young in Paradox, Colorado. Siringo was about two weeks behind Harvey Logan and another man, believed to be Bill Cruzan. The third robber, Ben Kilpatrick, had apparently doubled back north.

In the Blue Mountains west of Monticello, Utah – known today as the Abajo Mountains – Siringo fell in with local outlaws, including a one-time sheriff he identified only as Bill G., and another man whom Siringo referred to as "Peg-leg." The latter had visited the Tipton train robbers in their camp, and he told Siringo they were still heading south. Peg-leg and Siringo surreptitiously visited Monticello, where they met other outlaws who told them a Pinkerton agent was rumored to be tracking the train bandits. They didn't suspect Siringo.

Initially, Siringo believed Logan, or Kid Curry, was the leader of the Wild Bunch. But, in the midst of his chase for Logan and Cruzan, Siringo's supervisor ordered him to search near the hometown of Robert LeRoy Parker, better known as Butch Cassidy, at Circleville, Utah. Siringo soon realized Cassidy was the true leader. Cassidy, he wrote, "turned out to be the shrewdest and most daring outlaw of the present age, though not of the blood-spilling kind like 'Kid' Curry."

From Circleville, Siringo traveled to Alma, New Mexico, a ranching community near the Arizona border, where members of the Wild Bunch were known to hide out. There his frustration grew significantly because of the actions of a fellow detective. Frank Murray, a Pinkerton man from Denver, had been in Alma the previous year, looking for the men who held up another train in Wilcox, Wyoming, in 1899. Murray had revealed his identity to a local bar owner named Jim Lowe, Siringo said. The problem was, Jim Lowe was really Butch Cassidy, who soon warned his colleagues. On top of that, Siringo said, some of the bandits wanted to kill Murray once they learned his identity. But Lowe/Cassidy saved Murray's life, sneaking him out of town at night. Then Cassidy sold his saloon and skipped town as well. If not for Murray's missteps, Siringo believed he could have rounded up much of the Wild Bunch near Alma.

From Alma, Siringo returned to Denver, and was again sent to Grand Junction. There, using the alias Lee Roy Davis, he met Jim Ferguson, a Wild Bunch affiliate then living in nearby Palisade, Colorado. Although Ferguson was not seen as an active train and bank robber with the Wild Bunch, the Pinkerton Agency believed he supplied horses to the Tipton train bandits, as well as a place to hide out at his ranch near Dixon, Wyoming. He was also a convicted cattle thief who had spent time in the South Dakota state prison.

By 1902, Ferguson had moved to Palisade, where he remained for 11 years, operating a pool hall and saloon and serving briefly as town marshal. A Pinkerton report said he claimed his occupation was carpentry, but his criminal resume included "thief, rustler and associate of train robbers."

Over the next three years, Siringo spent time in Rawlins, Wyoming, traveled back to Palisade, then south to Santa Fe, New Mexico to deliver a coded letter from Butch Cassidy to Elzy Lay, Cassidy's good friend, who was then in prison in New Mexico. He made several more trips to Palisade, Rawlins, northern Wyoming, and Utah.

Ferguson never tumbled to the fact that Lee Roy Davis was actually Pinkerton Agent Charlie Siringo, even though on one occasion he received a letter telling him a Pinkerton Agent was on the trail of the Wild Bunch. Upon reading the letter, Ferguson swore and proclaimed to Davis/Siringo that he "would cut out the heart of any detective who undertook to win his friendship." The unflappable Siringo stood quietly listening to Ferguson.

Siringo later claimed that the Pinkerton Agency learned the identity of the Sundance Kid – Harry Longabaugh – from the conversations Siringo had with the loquacious Ferguson.

While he was on the trail of the Tipton bandits, Siringo also visited Gunnison, Colorado, and courted the sister of an outlaw to obtain more information on the Wild Bunch. He abandoned that relationship when she proposed marriage.

Finally, in the fall of 1904, Siringo returned to Denver and ended his Tipton quest. By then, he wrote, the Wild Bunch had largely ceased to exist. "The only two really 'bad' ones who escaped were 'Butch' Casiday [Cassidy] and Harry Longbough [Longabaugh]." They had fled to South America in 1901, along with Longabaugh's girlfriend, Ethel or Etta Place. By late 1904, Cruzan had disappeared and Kilpatrick was in prison. Kid Curry was thought to have been killed in the aftermath of the June 1904 train robbery near Parachute, Colorado, although Siringo and others with the Pinkerton Agency believed he somehow survived and escaped to South America.

After he quit the Pinkertons in 1907, Siringo retired to a ranch near Santa Fe, where he wrote several more books. He moved to Los Angeles in the 1920s and became friends with people like Will Rogers and artist Charles Russell. He served as an adviser for several Hollywood Westerns. He died in Los Angeles in 1928.

Sources: "A Cowboy Detective," by Charles A. Siringo; "Charlie Siringo's West," by Howard R. Lamar; Pinkerton Agency Reports provided by Wild Bunch Historian Bob Goodwin, Pleasant Grove, Utah; historic newspapers at www.newspapers.com and www.colorado-historicnewspapers.org.

PART SEVEN: TRAVEL TENDENCIES

GJ Train – An early Denver and Rio Grande Railroad train sitting outside the depot at Grand Junction, Colorado. Date unknown. *Image courtesy of the Museums of Western Colorado.*

CAMERON'S R.R. TICKET A

TAKE this CAR
GRAND HOT

e Pill CURE NERVOUS DISORDERS.
HASKELL'S PHARMACY,
SOLE AGENTS.

o BANNISTER Furniture
For and UNDERTAKING

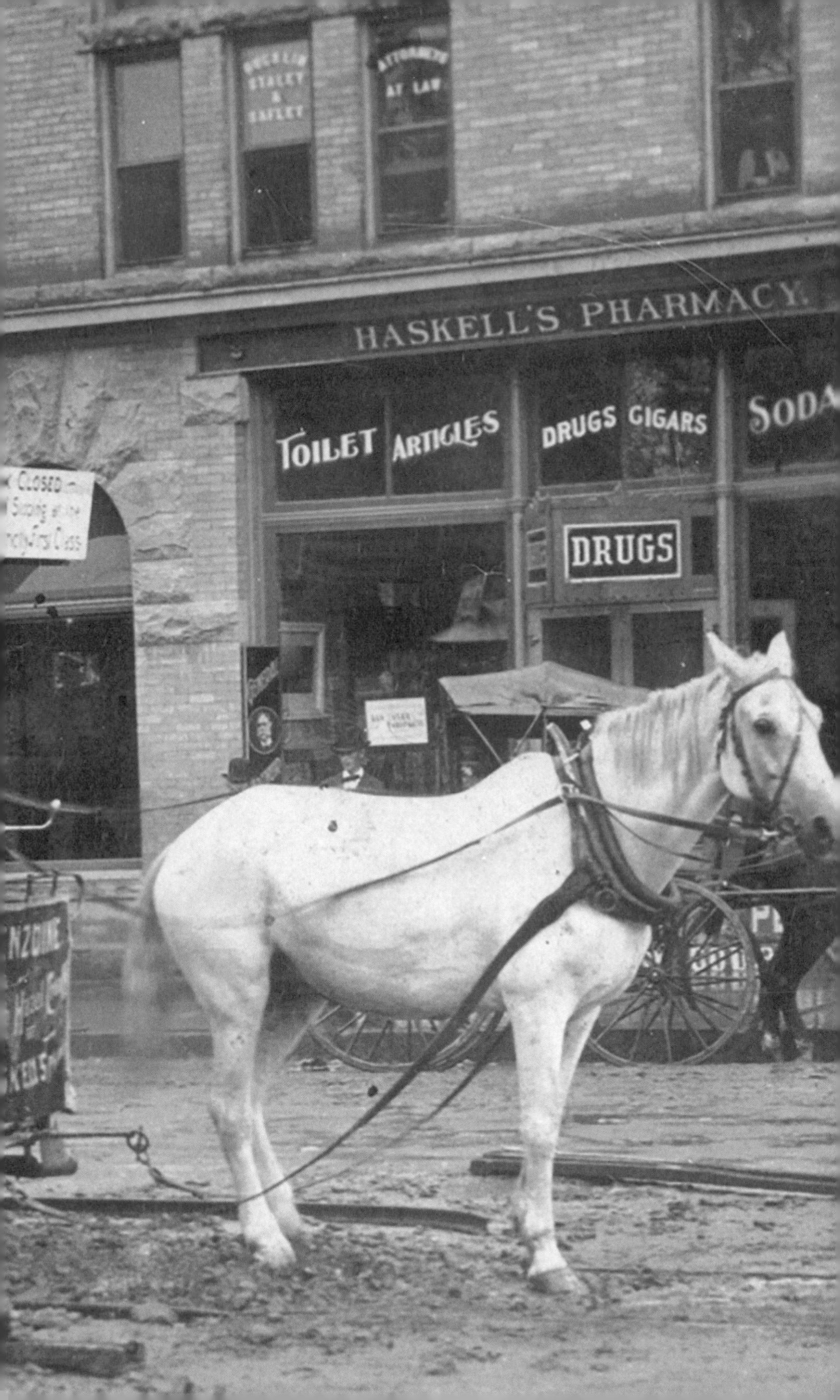
ATTORNEYS AT LAW
HASKELL'S PHARMACY.
TOILET ARTICLES
DRUGS CIGARS
SODA
DRUGS
CLOSED

CHAPTER 32:
EUROPEAN EXPLORERS FOLLOWED
LONG-USED NATIVE ROUTES

On August 26, 1776, after descending the eastern side of the Uncompahgre Plateau to the Uncompahgre River Valley near present-day Montrose, Colorado, Father Francisco Silvestre Vélez de Escalante wrote, "In the meadow of this river ... there is a very wide and well-beaten trail."

With Father Francisco Atanasio Domínguez, Escalante led a six-month expedition from Santa Fe, New Mexico, into lands that are now part of Colorado, Utah and Arizona. They were ostensibly looking for a good route from Santa Fe to California, but they also wanted to meet Natives, make converts to Catholicism, and look for areas where more Spaniards might settle.

In his diary of the expedition, Escalante made it clear they trod on trails long used by Native Americans in the region. For instance, on September 9, led by a Ute guide, the expedition descended the north side of Douglas Pass toward today's Rangely, Colorado. Escalante wrote that the group traveled nearly 30 miles "over a very well-beaten trail with only one bad stretch." Since few, if any, Europeans had traveled this region before Dominguez and Escalante, this "well-beaten trail" was established by the Natives who lived there. In 1776, that meant the Utes and Comanches. But the trails were likely used by a variety of Native people over the ages.

It wasn't just Spanish explorers who used Native travel routes. Nineteenth century American explorers such as John Fremont and Kit Carson, along with numerous fur traders, followed routes established long before by Native Americans.

"Lots of people used these areas," said Carl Conner, owner of Grand River Institute, an archaeological consulting firm in Grand Junction, Colorado. He is also founder of the Dominquez Archaeological Research Group, or DARG, an associated nonprofit organization.

Conner noted that in the Piceance Basin north of Parachute, Colorado, archaeologists have found many items from the Utes who once lived in the re-

Photo on previous page: Horse trolley – Frank Catalina and his horse, Charlie, offered public transportation in downtown Grand Junction, Colorado, in the 1890s. *Image courtesy of the Museums of Western Colorado.*

gion. But Conner and his team have also found evidence that members of the Fremont Culture, which predated the Utes, as well as more recent visitors such as Shoshones and Navajos, visited the Piceance Basin. And there are traces of Dismal River culture, believed to be the Apaches' ancestors.

Beyond the Piceance Basin, archaeologists in Western Colorado have found shell beads that originated on the Pacific Coast and obsidian that came from Wyoming, New Mexico, and other parts of Colorado. Clearly, many people moved through this region, whether trading, traveling, or relocating. They certainly had numerous long-established routes.

Through DARG, Conner and Project Coordinator Richard Ott have undertaken the Ute Trails Project, attempting to trace major Western Colorado trails. "We wanted to take more of a landscape approach rather than just a site-by-site look," Conner explained. "We wanted to try to discern how these sites relate to each other with trails."

One such trail is the path taken by Dominguez and Escalante in 1776, when they were led by Ute guides over long-used trails. On another route, from Southern Wyoming, south past Brown's Park in Northwestern Colorado, then on toward the Piceance Basin, the researchers found water holes roughly every 25 miles. That makes sense for people on horseback, who needed regular water stops for their animals, Ott said. That particular route may have been used by Utes who traveled north to raid for horses, then returned to their own territory with the stolen animals.

Water availability also was key to another route Conner and Ott investigated on the advice of modern Ute leaders. It went from the Dolores River south of Gateway, Colorado, over the relatively dry Uncompahgre Plateau to the Gunnison River near Big Dominguez Canyon. Horseback riders could make the trip in a day, ensuring they had water at each end of the journey.

It's not just rivers. Mountain passes, many of which today accommodate modern highways, were also used long ago by Utes and others. "Every mountain pass that's worth a hill of beans has (an archaeological) site of some sort on it," said John Goodwin, who spent much of his career doing archaeological work for Colorado highway projects. On some passes, artifacts dating back thousands of years have been discovered. Others show only more recent inhabitation or visitation. Colorado mountain passes that showed evidence of early visitation include Vail Pass, Cerro Summit east of Montrose, Cottonwood Pass near Glenwood Springs, Cochetopa Pass into the San Luis Valley and Ute Pass, which connected Colorado Springs to South Park.

Historian Celinda R. Kaelin said the Ute Pass trail "was of great importance to the Ute Indians as it was one of their major 'salt roads.'" It connected the salt beds in South Park to the trading centers at Taos and Santa Fe, she wrote. Moreover, the trail was likely used for thousands of years prior to the

Chaco Road 2 – Upper Kin Klizhin, in Northern New Mexico, a structure south of Chaco Canyon on the ancient Chaco Road. *Historic American Buildings Survey, Library of Congress.*

19th century. Prehistoric projectile points 10,000 years old have been found at the Florissant Fossil Beds on the west side of Ute Pass.

Perhaps no prehistoric trail in the Southwest is as famous as the Chaco Meridian, or Chaco Road, which runs almost arrow-straight from Aztec, New Mexico, south through the Chaco Canyon complex in New Mexico, then farther south to a prehistoric site in Sonora, Mexico.

University of Colorado archaeologist and author Stephen H. Lekson has detailed how the people of the Chacoan culture could have surveyed the road, built about a thousand years ago, with only a few degrees of error using the tools they had available to them. Archaeologists have long known trade occurred between southern parts of Mexico and places like Chaco. Macaw and parrot feathers, as well as copper and beads from far to the south have been found at Chaco and related sites.

Although many ancient routes became horse trails, wagon roads, and eventually highways, not all Native trails evolved that way. People on foot could go up and over obstacles far easier than those pulling wagons or even riding horseback. As Lekson put it: "Pueblo trails and Chacoan roads, whether symbolic or functional, were not bridle paths ... Wagon roads, developed for new transportation technologies, may not represent the most important ancient routes."

With that in mind, archaeologists know there were well-used old trails, such as the Navajo-Uncompahgre Trail, which ran north out of New Mexico and onto the Uncompahgre Plateau, that never became major routes for wagons or autos. Another well-documented route ran across the Flat Tops from the Colorado River near Dotsero, Colorado, to the White River near today's town of Meeker, Colorado. It was used by Utes and others. But it never developed beyond a horse trail, perhaps because the rugged terrain made building a wagon road too difficult. Similarly, the majority of a 19th century route from the Los Piños Indian Agency in the Uncompahgre River Valley to the White River Agency near present-day Meeker, highlighted on Hayden Survey maps from 1877, remained only a horse trail.

Even with the work of Conner, Ott, and people like Lekson, it's impossible to identify all the ancient pathways. But there is a growing understanding among researchers that, whether riding horses or trekking on foot, this region's early inhabitants had their own network of long-used routes and "well-beaten trails" as intricate as any modern highway system.

Sources: Author interviews with Carl Connor, Richard Ott and John Goodwin; "The Chaco Meridian," by Stephen H. Lekson; "Pikes Peak Backcountry," by Celinda Reynolds Kaelin, at www.academia.edu; "Juan Rivera's Colorado, 1765," by Steven G. Baker; "Pageant in the Wilderness," by Herbert E. Bolton.

CHAPTER 33:
'LINKED AT LAST:' RAILROAD REACHED
GRAND JUNCTION, SALT LAKE

———

The Grand Junction News was ecstatic when it reported the arrival of the first Denver & Rio Grande Railroad train in Grand Junction, Colorado, at seven minutes before 5 p.m. on November 21, 1882. "Tuesday will be remembered in the history of Grand Junction as the day which united us by two steel rails with all parts of the United States," the newspaper declared under the headline: "Linked at Last."

For others in Colorado and in Utah, however, the Grand Junction connection was just one more step in the greater effort to establish a rail link from Denver to Salt Lake City through the heart of Western Colorado. The most difficult section of that effort involved blasting and building the railroad through a portion of the Black Canyon of the Gunnison River, east of today's Montrose, Colorado. When surveyors for the railroad told D&RG founder General William Jackson Palmer that it was impossible to build through the canyon, the determined Palmer hired new surveyors. They began work in January 1881.

"The surveying was extremely dangerous and was done partially through the use of ropes and scaling ladders," wrote historian Duane Vandenbusche. In particularly narrow sections, "Men, horses, and wagons were lowered down the steep walls by ropes." One member of the surveying party was killed when the rope he was using to scale the canyon wall broke. Wrote Vandenbusche: "The daring engineer was dashed to death at the bottom of the cañon."

Despite such obstacles, the surveyors finished their work by summer 1881. And this time the report to Palmer was acceptable: A railroad could be built through the eastern end of the Black Canyon, but it would have to come out where the Cimarron River enters the canyon to flow into the Gunnison River. There, the railroad would continue westward over Cerro Summit and on to the Uncompahgre Valley, the surveyors said.

Construction in the canyon began that summer and, Vandenbusche wrote, "For a year, over one thousand men blasted and cut a road bed fifteen miles through the gorge." Those 15 miles now lie under the waters of Morrow Point Reservoir.

The Black Canyon had some of the most stunning vistas on the picturesque D&RG mountain route. Mrs. W.B. Wilson Jr., who in 1890 traveled through the canyon en route from California to South Carolina, wrote, "This is considered the finest scenery on the Continent."

British author Rudyard Kipling painted a gripping and terrifying word picture of the trip after he rode the D&RG through the Black Canyon in 1889: "Then the driver put on all the steam and we would go round the curve on one wheel chiefly, the Gunnison River gnashing its teeth below. The cars overhung the edge of the water, and if a single one of the rails had chosen to spread, nothing in the wide world could have saved us from drowning."

Once the Black Canyon route was completed, construction continued westward in late 1882 – to Montrose and Delta, Colorado, then finally, to Grand Junction in November. On the day the first train steamed into town, "a party of ladies and gentlemen from Grand Junction walked across the bridge" over the Grand River, now called the Colorado. The final work on the bridge had been completed just an hour earlier. Then the town dignitaries, led by Grand Junction founder George Crawford, rode the first train back across the bridge and into Grand Junction.

News reports in 1882 predicted the final link between Denver and Salt Lake would be completed by January 1, 1883. But the date was pushed back to February, then March. The first passenger train actually made the full 735-mile journey from Denver to Salt Lake City in April, 1883. For comparison's sake, a 21st century highway trip between the two cities is about 525 miles. Even so, the railroad trip was far better than the horse-and-wagon alternative. Little wonder that a Delta, Colorado, newspaper hailed the achievement of finishing the Denver-to-Salt Lake City line: "The completion of the Utah extension marks an epoch in the history of the West," it said. The event would allow Western Colorado, "to be the food furnisher for a large part of the mountain country."

With the completion of the railroad link, the *Grand Junction News* predicted a great future for Grand Junction. It would lead to a day when the small community "shall assume the proportions of a metropolis, and become a beautiful city; with delightful parks and drives, handsome residences, immense manufactories, machine shops and smelters," the paper said.

While other papers around the state weren't quite as effusive, they also saw the community's potential. "With its enjoyable climate and advantageous surroundings, its prosperous future seems to be assured," the *Leadville Daily Herald* wrote on November 30, 1882. To take advantage of that sentiment in cold, high-elevation Leadville, the D&RG arranged for an excursion train from Leadville to Grand Junction, providing both sightseeing opportunities and a chance for visitors to assess the newer town's development potential. The train left Leadville early on December 21, 1882, and arrived in Grand Junction near midnight that night.

One unnamed participant on the excursion said about 100 people boarded the train at Leadville, and more got on at stops in Salida and Gunnison. Few came simply to see the sights, the anonymous author told the *Herald*. "Nearly all were bound on a practical voyage of investigation, with an eye to business." The enthusiastic author concluded, "I consider the purchase of a quarter section of land in Grand River valley [surrounding Grand Junction] as a better and safer investment than double the number of acres in Iowa and Minnesota, those boasted gardens of the west."

The railroad's arrival in Grand Junction was definitely a great event, and the *Grand Junction News* gave appropriate credit to William Palmer's vision. "Three cheers for the little Denver & Rio Grande," it exhorted. "No obstacles stand in its way."

No physical ones, perhaps, but financial obstacles were another matter. "The reward for the gritty, focused work of engineers and crews and the determination of Palmer in creating a Denver-to-Pacific link was financial failure," wrote the authors of a history of Colorado's railroads. The D&RG's rapid track laying on a variety of routes combined with an economic downturn spelled temporary disaster. Both the D&RG and its Utah sister, the Denver & Rio Grande Western, went into receivership in 1884. When they emerged two years later, Palmer had regained control and he pushed to widen the tracks from narrow-gauge to standard.

In late 1890, working with the Colorado Midland Railroad, the D&RG completed a shorter connection between Denver and Grand Junction, bringing standard-gauge tracks west from Aspen to Glenwood Springs, then down river to the Grand Valley. Until that occurred, travelers had to use the longer, narrow-gauge route between Grand Junction and Denver that went through Delta, Montrose, the Black Canyon, and Gunnison, Colorado, then over Marshal Pass to the east side of the Continental Divide, through the Royal Gorge to Pueblo, then north to Denver. Mrs. Wilson, who had been excited about the Black Canyon, was even more ecstatic about the Royal Gorge: "This was the very cream of our trip," she wrote. "Imagination cannot conceive of such scenes as those wild rocks towering from 1,000 to 3,000 feet skyward." She exaggerated a bit. At its deepest point, the canyon walls of the Royal Gorge are 1,200 feet high.

Still, Palmer and his staff recognized the importance of the spectacular Colorado landscape, even as they fought to build rail lines across the rugged ground. From its earliest days, the D&RG included observation cars and sightseeing excursions and proclaimed itself the "Scenic Line of the World."

Sources: Colorado historic newspapers at www.newspapers.com and www.coloradohis-toricnewspapers.org; Utah historic newspapers at www.digitalnewspapers.org; "Man Against the Black Canyon," by Duane Vandenbusche, Colorado Magazine, Spring 1973; "Notes on a Western Tour," by Mrs. W.B. Wilson Jr.; "Railroads in Colorado 1858-1948," by Clayton B. Fraser and Jennifer H. Strand; "Rio Grande: Mainline of the Rockies," by Lucius Beebe and Charles Clegg.

CHAPTER 34:
INTERURBAN STREETCAR KEPT FRUITA
AND GRAND JUNCTION CONNECTED

———

Real estate in Fruita, Colorado, suddenly became a hot commodity early in 1910. Residents of Grand Junction, Colorado, ten miles to the east, were anticipating the opening of an electric rail system called the Fruit Belt Route between Grand Junction and Fruita. The electric train, commonly called the Interurban, would make it possible for people to live in Fruita and commute to Grand Junction.

"There was the damnedest land boom in Fruita you ever saw," recalled savings and loan executive Howard McMullin of Grand Junction decades later. "They were building houses like mad down there." A price war between local lumber yards helped fuel the boom, he added. And the lumber could be shipped to Fruita on the Interurban. McMullin was a boy when the route opened, but worked with some of the mortgage holders after he joined the firm of Home Loan and Investment in the 1920s.

Grand Junction was only nine years old when its first horse-drawn streetcar line began operating in September 1890. The firm, originally called the Grand Junction Street Car Co., reorganized and changed ownership several times over the next decade. In 1900, the city of Grand Junction purchased all the equipment and the few blocks of track on which the streetcars operated. It then solicited bids for the operation of the system, and an African American named John Price won the contract to operate the streetcars for fifteen dollars a month.

The city renewed the contract with Price the next two years. But sometime in autumn 1902, Price stopped operating the streetcar line after an extremely hot summer that took a serious toll on the horses he used to pull the streetcars. Early the next year, the city decided to abandon the system and ordered the streetcar tracks to be removed.

It wasn't until six years later, in May 1909, that electric streetcars began operating in Grand Junction. It took another year to complete the 12-mile, zig-zag connection to Fruita. But with that link, suddenly the sky seemed the limit for connecting Mesa County communities. Nearly everyone believed that an electric streetcar running east 10 miles to Palisade was a foregone conclusion. Beyond Palisade, there were plans to extend the electric line up Plateau Creek to the ranching communities of Mesa and Collbran, Colorado.

Apple Streetcar – Workers gather apples as the Interurban trolley from Grand Junction to Fruita, Colorado passes by, circa 1910. *Frank Dean photo, Library of Congress.*

A hydroelectric plant to provide power was contemplated in De Beque Canyon to the northeast, and there was talk of running the electric train line to the town of De Beque and beyond. To the west, it was planned that the electric line would eventually extend as far as Mack, Colorado and connect with the Uintah Railway that ran northwest into Utah.

None of these dreams materialized. But for nearly two decades, the Interurban provided steady electric train service between Grand Junction and Fruita. Students at Appleton School – about halfway between the two towns – could ride the line to and from classes for a nickel. Sports teams and their fans rode the electric cars to athletic contests in Fruita or Grand Junction. Special rates attracted riders during the Mesa County Fair each summer. Sightseeing trips were frequent to orchard lands prevalent west of Grand Junction early in the 20th century. Additionally, freight moved regularly between the two communities on the electric line: fruit at harvest time, agricultural supplies, building materials and more.

But Interurban finances were always shaky. Paved roads and improved motor vehicles eventually made the electric train superfluous. Passenger service on the Interurban halted in October, 1928. The Fruit Belt Route continued to haul fruit and other freight, but that ended on January 1, 1935.

However, the automobiles, trucks and busses that eventually supplanted the electric line were still novelties when a few Colorado men began envisioning electric streetcars for Mesa County in the early 1900s. Among those leading the charge was businessman and former Grand Junction Mayor Orson Adams. In 1908, he joined four Colorado Springs men and a banker from Glenwood Springs to form the Fruit Belt Power and Irrigation Co. They hired an attorney who had previously served as treasurer of the Colorado Midland Railway to oversee finances and legal issues. Selling electricity and supplying power to irrigators was the group's original intent. Their proposed dam near De Beque was expected to produce enough power to light the homes, businesses and farms around Grand Junction while providing irrigation water to cultivate new lands.

The company soon changed its focus from irrigation and selling electricity to electric streetcars. By June 1908, it had announced that it would request a streetcar franchise from the Grand Junction City Council. The franchise was approved on July 17, 1908, with a requirement that the company have three miles of streetcar line in operation within a year. The franchise agreement allowed the company to operate the line for 25 years.

The company reorganized, and became the Grand Junction Electric Railway Co. By December 1908, steel rails were ordered, and in January 1909, a temporary agreement to provide electric power was signed with the Grand Junction Gas, Electric and Manufacturing Co. A large Westinghouse "railroad type generator" was installed at the electric plant. The last of the rails were laid on April 12, 1909, but work on overhead powerlines continued for another month.

The official opening for the electric streetcar line was Saturday, May 22, 1909, when five-year-old Edith Adams, the daughter of Orson Adams, pulled a lever that connected the generator to overhead electric lines. Two electric cars, each pulling another car, departed from the new car barn at 2 p.m., carrying company executives, city leaders, members of the Grand Junction Chamber of Commerce, newspaper reporters and others. The rest of the day, free rides were offered to anyone who wanted a lift. "Everybody cheered the cars, and handkerchiefs and hats were waved everywhere," *The Grand Junction Daily Sentinel* reported the next day.

Even as that grand opening of the city line was held, efforts were underway to extend the electric line to other parts of Mesa County. The company was reorganized again as the Grand Junction and Grand River Valley Railway Co., and it purchased the local electric plant. Talk continued of pushing east toward Palisade and beyond, but right-of-way acquisition became a serious obstacle. Soon, folks in Fruita realized that if they could overcome those sorts of problems, they could have the first extension outside Grand Junction. People to the west began pledging to provide rights of way for the Interurban, and the company responded.

By the end of November 1909, company General Manager and Vice President Eugene Sunderlin announced that the firm was ready to build the line to Fruita. Rather than a straight run, the line would zigzag through the farm country between the two municipalities and would be in operation by June 1910, he said. Construction crews didn't quite meet that deadline, but they worked rapidly, nonetheless.

Beginning in early March 1910, they had built the streetcar line north from downtown Grand Junction, then northwest into the outlying farmlands. Another crew built a yellow brick building in Fruita, the western terminus of the line. Wooden trestles were built over canals and washes. Overhead lines were installed along the route, and an electric locomotive to pull freight cars arrived in early June.

Finally, on July 14, 1910, the Interurban opened to passenger travel between the two towns. An estimated 7,000 people gathered in Fruita to celebrate the arrival of the first electric cars from Grand Junction. There were speeches, bands, baseball games, a barbecue, and a parade. "On this day, July 14, 1910, is opened for operation one of the most modern and fully equipped interurban railways in the West," the *Sentinel* announced.

In an editorial, the newspaper added, "We believe this is the entering wedge only of what may become a great system of interurban electric road penetrating to all portions of western Colorado." That did not occur, but for 18 years, the

Fruit Belt Route, or Interurban, provided a critical passenger connection between Grand Junction and Fruita.

Sources: "The Fruit Belt Route: The Railways of Grand Junction, Colorado, 1890-1935," by William L. McGuire and Charles Teed; "Historic Streetcar Systems of Colorado," by Nick VanderKwaak, Jennifer Wahlers, Dianna Litvak and Ethan Raath, for the Colorado Department of Transportation; historic editions of The Daily Sentinel through www.newspapers.com.

CHAPTER 35:
DOUGLAS PASS HIGHWAY PROVIDED
A KEY LINK TO UINTAH BASIN

On July 4, 1924, thirty automobiles carrying more than 100 people from Mesa County, Colorado, rolled into Vernal, Utah, just in time for that town's holiday festivities. Their primary purpose, however, was to celebrate the completion of an auto road from the Grand Valley in Colorado to the Uintah Basin in Utah over Douglas Pass. The pass cuts through the long line of the Book Cliffs that extend from Western Colorado into Eastern Utah. It was named for a White River Ute leader named Douglas.

The exultation over the new road did not last long, however. The Colorado Highway Department regularly neglected the road in coming years. In 1948, the state's top highway engineer declared he would not "spend one cent" on Douglas Pass. It was not until the 1960s that the state agreed to give the road, now known as Colorado Highway 139, the attention it needed.

The road celebrated in 1924 was the result of a concerted fundraising and lobbying effort by the Grand Junction Chamber of Commerce and Grand Junction Rotary Club. The groups obtained additional support from Mesa County, as well as from officials in Vernal, Utah, and Garfield County, Colorado. That support was not just for the road connection. The route over Douglas Pass offered new economic opportunities for Western Colorado and Northeastern Utah, as well as better connections to the outside world for the Uintah Basin. In a special edition on July 3, 1924, *The Daily Sentinel* of Grand Junction said the new road was "expected to save people in the Uintah Basin millions of dollars and to bring millions of dollars' worth of business" to Western Colorado.

Although automobiles were new to Douglas Pass in 1924, people had been traveling on something close to this route since before recorded history. Spanish explorers Fray Francisco Atanasio Domínguez and Fray Francisco Silvestre Vélez de Escalante journeyed over the Book Cliffs near today's Douglas Pass and down Douglas Creek in 1776, guided by Ute Indians whose ancestors had been using the trail for centuries. Additionally, maps from the late 19th century show a wagon road from Fruita, Colorado, to Rangely, Colorado, topping the Book Cliffs near Douglas Pass.

In the early 20th century, however, the primary connection between Grand Junction and Vernal was over Baxter Pass on the Uintah Railway to Dragon, Utah. From Dragon, 50 miles of travel on a wagon road were required to reach

Coltharp Truck -- J.H. Coltharp of Rangely, Colorado, delivered alfalfa seed over the new Vernal, Utah, to Grand Junction, Colorado road, circa 1924. He is driving for White Bus and Truck Line of Grand Junction, which began service over Douglas Pass in June 1924. *Used by permission, Uintah County Library Regional History Center. All rights reserved.*

Vernal. Alternatively, one could drive the rough road west from Grand Junction by way of Cisco, Green River and Price, Utah, then follow more than 100 miles of rugged road to Vernal. The route was impassable in winter. Or one could drive east from Grand Junction to Rifle, Colorado, go north to Meeker on a rough dirt road, then west to Rangely on equally rough roads before continuing northeast to Vernal.

To Grand Junction and Vernal business leaders, these alternatives were inadequate. They saw the possibility of cutting the automobile distance by nearly 100 miles compared to the Price, Utah, route, or more than 60 miles compared to the Meeker road, while improving both commerce and comity between the two communities. So, in 1919, people in Grand Junction and Vernal began stumping for an auto road to connect the regions. They also wanted a better link to the newly developing oil fields around Rangely.

In June 1919, after an investigative trip by business leaders, it was determined that constructing a road north from Loma, Colorado, then over the Book Cliffs via Douglas Pass to the Douglas Creek drainage and on into Rangely would be the best route. At Rangely, the new road would connect with the existing road from Meeker to Vernal.

By September 1919, Uintah Basin citizens had approved $60,000 in bonds to improve their section of road from the Utah-Colorado line west to Vernal and on to Roosevelt, Utah. The Colorado effort moved more slowly. Even so, by March 1920, both the Grand Junction Chamber of Commerce and the year-old Rotary Club had created committees to support the road project and to raise money. *The Daily Sentinel* also backed the project.

Within a year, the two Grand Junction organizations had raised more than $30,000, and officials in Garfield County, Colorado, had committed an unspecified amount to complete a portion of the road. The Colorado State Road Commission agreed to make the route a unit of the state highway system and contributed several thousand dollars for its construction.

However, not everyone supported the project. A newspaper in Price noted that Grand Junction had raised money for the new road, but questioned whether "the merchants and shippers of the Vernal district will really gain anything" from it. The paper also complained that the state of Utah had not done enough to improve the road west from Cisco to Price.

In 1922, Garfield County, Colorado officials apparently had second thoughts about the new road. Working with officials from Meeker, they set up a tourist facility in Rifle, urging auto travelers to take the Meeker route to Vernal. Additionally, Garfield and Rio Blanco county officials protested to Colorado's governor about the possibility of the new Douglas Pass road being made a state highway.

Also in autumn 1922, business groups in Salt Lake City took note of the new road efforts. They began pushing for additional state and federal highway funds to improve roads between the Uintah Basin and Salt Lake rather than the Douglas Pass route.

Despite these efforts, the Douglas Pass road was largely completed by late 1923, and it was fully opened in time for the 1924 Fourth of July celebration in Vernal. Earlier that summer, the White Bus Line of Grand Junction began operating buses and freight trucks over Douglas Pass to Vernal. It seemed the new road was on track to provide exactly the sort of interstate connection that leaders in both the Uintah Basin and the Grand Valley had sought. But there was trouble ahead.

Three years later, the Douglas Pass road had deteriorated significantly, and the *Sentinel* urged local officials to push the Colorado Highway Department to make improvements. With pressure from Mesa County officials, some work eventually did occur. Still, state highway officials remained unsupportive. They eventually dropped the route from the list of Colorado highways and stopped funding maintenance.

In 1966, almost 50 years after its first effort began, the Grand Junction Rotary Club again took up the Douglas Pass cause. Working with the Western Slope promotional group Club 20, the Grand Junction Chamber of Commerce, and Mesa County officials, they got the state to commit $75,000 toward Douglas Pass improvements. The highway up the south side of the pass was realigned to reduce its grade and the tightness of its switchbacks. Also, the highway was paved. Finally, the connection over Douglas Pass had become permanent.

Even in the 21st century, however, the highway remains troublesome. It was closed for three days in March 2021 because of avalanche danger. Snowdrifts and rockslides had closed it several times in prior years. Wildfires have also closed the road and increased the possibility of mudslides in burned areas. But the state is no longer neglecting the road. In 2020 the Colorado Department of Transportation completed a resurfacing project on the south side of Douglas Pass.

Today, more than a century after it was first proposed, Highway 139 over Douglas Pass remains the quickest auto route between the Grand Valley and the Uintah Basin. The drive from Grand Junction to Vernal that took eight hours in 1924, can now be accomplished in three hours.

Sources: Colorado historic newspapers at www.newspapers.com and Utah historic newspapers at www.digitalnewspapers.org; the Museums of Western Colorado; The Uintah County Regional History Center, Vernal, Utah; "Douglas Pass," by Herb Bacon, Grand Junction Rotary 50th anniversary edition; Colorado Department of Transportation, www.cdot.gov.

PART EIGHT:
OUTDOORS CALLING

Harold Guesburg bike – Harold Guesburg, of Grand Junction, Colorado, in Glenwood Springs, Colorado, after winning Basalt to Glenwood race circa 1915. *Courtesy of Chris Brown, Brown Cycles.*

CHAPTER 36:
NATURAL WILDLIFE PHOTOGRAPHY
BORN IN NORTHWESTERN COLORADO

———

A.G. Wallihan lugged his heavy box camera and tripod down a steep trail into Juniper Canyon on the Yampa River in the spring of 1891. There he took one of the earliest photos ever made of a wild animal in a natural setting. "I sat upright on the gravelly edge of the river, without anything to hide me," Wallihan wrote in his 1894 book of unstaged wildlife photos – perhaps the first such book ever published. "A yearling doe came down and after drinking and satisfying herself that everything was right she started over. When about twenty steps from shore, she turned to land above me and I took a snap shot while [she was] swimming."

In today's age when smartphones make snapping quick photos and videos of wildlife routine – and social media allow them to be seen by thousands of viewers in a heartbeat – it's difficult to comprehend how hard it was to capture wildlife on film before the turn of the last century. The swimming deer wasn't Wallihan's first wildlife photo. He acquired his heavy box camera in 1889, and he took a photo of several mule deer in 1890. But the photo of the deer swimming was published first, and it helped ignite a movement among photographers globally to capture pictures of wildlife in their natural habitats.

Prior to the 1890s, wildlife photos were usually staged – often animals stuffed by taxidermists and set in lifelike poses. In the late 1880s and early 1890s, new cameras and lenses became available, including George Eastman's small, handheld camera.

It's not clear who took the first photos of animals in the wild. George Shiras III began taking wildlife photos in Michigan's Upper Peninsula in 1889 or 1890. Unlike Wallihan, he snapped his photos mostly at night using a flash, often setting up a trip wire so the animals would snap their own photos. In England, brothers Richard and Cherry Kearton began taking natural shots of insects and birds in their nests in the early 1890s. However, famed zoologist William Hornaday had no doubt who deserved the honor. He believed A.G. Wallihan was "the first man in the world to take pictures of wild animals in their native habitat."

Wallihan was a self-taught photographer who favored box cameras and tripods over the newer, smaller cameras. He was also the postmaster in tiny Lay, Colorado, about 20 miles west of Craig, Colorado. His wife Augusta joined him

Deer swim – A doe swims the Bear (now known as the Yampa) River in this 1891 photograph by A.G. Wallihan of Lay, Colorado, perhaps the earliest photograph published of wildlife in its natural habitat. *Courtesy of the Museum of Northwest Colorado, Downtown Craig, Colorado.*

in many of his photographic endeavors. Both were also crack shots with rifles. A.G. and Augusta Wallihan were born and raised in Wisconsin. But they didn't meet until they moved to the West.

Allen Grant Wallihan arrived in Colorado permanently in 1876, living first in Leadville, then Colorado Springs, before heading to the Western Slope. In 1882, he homesteaded on land in Brown's Park in the state's northwest corner. Three years later, he homesteaded on land in what would become Lay, not far from Brown's Park. Also in 1885, he was named postmaster for Lay, a position he held until his death in 1935. When he died, he was the longest-serving postmaster in Colorado, and the sixth longest in the United States, according to *The Steamboat Pilot* newspaper.

Mary Augusta Higgins was born near Milwaukee 22 years before A.G. She married a Civil War veteran, and they eventually moved west, traveling in an ox cart to Denver, then to Salt Lake City, according to Dan Davidson, director of the Museum of Northwest Colorado in Craig. Augusta's first husband drank heavily, however, and she divorced him in Utah, then moved to Brown's Park with her brother. There she met A.G. Wallihan and they were married in 1885. A.G. grew his long beard to mask the age difference between himself and his wife.

In addition to running the Lay post office, the couple operated a telegraph

AG Walli – A.G. Wallihan, considered by many as the father of natural wildlife photography, with his box camera near his home at Lay, Colorado. Date unknown. *Courtesy of the Museum of Northwest Colorado, Downtown Craig, Colorado.*

office, boarding house, and farm. In 1889, Augusta encouraged her husband to attempt to photograph some of the wildlife near their home. They traded for a box camera, and A.G. taught himself how to take photos and produce pictures from negatives. Before long, Augusta was accompanying him on his photographic expeditions, and she began taking photos of her own.

They soon found a fan for their work in an up-and-coming politician from New York: Theodore Roosevelt. In an introduction to the Wallihans' 1894 book of photos, Roosevelt wrote, "It has never been my good fortune to see as interesting a collection of game pictures as those that have been taken by Mr. and Mrs. Wallihan." Their book, he declared, was "absolutely unique."

Roosevelt remained friends with the Wallihans for years, even having them visit the White House when he was president. The Wallihans' photos may have persuaded Roosevelt to make two famous hunting trips to Western Colorado – one in 1901 when he was vice-president- elect, and one in 1905 while he was president. Roosevelt's introduction to Wallihan's second book, written in 1901, noted the many improvements in wildlife photography since 1894. He added, "Even under favorable conditions, very few men have the skill, the patience, the woodcraft and the plainscraft which enabled Mr. Wallihan to accomplish so much."

But Wallihan's expertise came through trial and error, and it advanced sporadically. In his second book, Wallihan described taking his first natural wildlife photo of several mule deer along the White River in October 1890. "I returned home, and upon developing the negative was elated to find it a good one – the first successful exposure I had ever made in my game series." But he did not obtain another good photo until the following spring, when he captured the doe swimming the Yampa River, then known as the Bear River. After that, he wrote, "A year or two passed with but poor success." Eventually, he and Augusta huddled in a tent during a snowstorm along the Yampa, and spent much of the next day in freezing cold, seated behind rocks near the river until they finally obtained a clear photo of nearly 30 deer.

Their skills continued to improve, and they branched out, producing photos of elk, antelope and other creatures. A.G. accompanied a hunter from Meeker on mountain lion hunts and obtained numerous photos of cougars, including a stunning shot of a leaping lion that was on the title page of his second book. There were also bears, bobcats, coyotes, rabbits, sage hens and geese.

Their books were popular, and the couple's work won international recognition. In 1900, a collection of their photos won top honors at the Paris Exposition in France. The collection won a bronze medal at the 1904 St. Louis World's Fair. They also became outspoken conservationists, joining Roosevelt in decrying for-profit hunters who were decimating big-game herds.

But fame did not persuade the Wallihans to leave Lay, Colorado. They remained there the rest of their lives. Augusta died in 1922, and A.G. eventually remarried, this time to a woman 20 years his junior. He shaved his beard to appear younger. Even when he was ill in 1935, the 76-year-old Wallihan refused to go to the hospital in Craig for treatment. "I've lived here for far the greater part of my life and here is where I want to die if my time has come," he told friends.

Sources: "Hoofs, claws and antlers of the Rocky Mountains," by Allen Grant Wallihan and Mary Augusta Higgins Wallihan; "Camera Shots at Big Game," by A.G. Wallihan; "The Wallihans – The world's first wildlife photographers," by Paul Knowles, Museum of Northwest Colorado, Craig Press, July 16, 2019; "A.G. Wallihan, Pioneer, Answers Final Summons," The Steamboat Pilot, December 20, 1935, at www.coloradohistoricnewspapers.org; "Theodore Roosevelt in Colorado," by Agnes Wright Spring, Colorado Magazine, October, 1958; Author interview with Dan Davidson, director, Museum of Northwest Colorado, Craig.

CHAPTER 37:
BICYCLING WAS A POPULAR PASTIME
IN EARLY COLORADO

An estimated 500 people gathered at Grand Junction, Colorado's railroad depot on June 4, 1897, along with two local bands, to greet a pair of hometown heroes. What had Alex Struthers and his uncle, William G. Struthers, done to deserve such acclaim? They'd won first and third places respectively in the 25-mile Decoration Day bicycle race in Denver, against some tough competition. As *The Daily Sentinel* in Grand Junction put it: "The victory, in the cycling world, was a great one." The annual race had attracted some of the top riders in the country, the paper said, but Alex Struthers had recorded the best time ever. "All honor to the victors," the *Sentinel* added.

In the still-small agricultural community of Grand Junction just before the turn of the 20th century, not everything was about fruit farming and ranching. Bicycling was already a popular activity. There were "wheel clubs" for cycling enthusiasts throughout Western Colorado in the early decades of settlement. Competing bike shops offered spare parts, repairs and the latest advancements in bicycle technology. Races – both short and long –attracted athletes like the Alex and William Struthers, as well as some of Grand Junction's civic leaders. Women joined the pedal brigades early, despite initial obstacles. There were also social rides, from Grand Junction to Palisade, to Fruita, to Whitewater, to Delta, and even to Glenwood Springs.

"I don't think cycling was just about cycling then," said Chris Brown, currently owner of Brown Cycles in Grand Junction and the author of the book, "Bicycle Junction." It was an important social activity. Groups such as the Denver Bicycling Club had their own building, he noted, with a bourbon room and an athletic room. Even smaller groups focused on social events. "Cycling was a piece of the aristocracy at the end of the Victorian era," before it became more affordable, Brown said. "The number of [Grand Junction] town founders who were on bikes is ridiculous," he added.

In addition to William G. Struthers, who became Mesa County Sheriff in 1902, there were people like Fred Mantey, for whom Mantey Heights in Grand Junction is named, and Samuel McMullin, founder of what is now Home Loan State Bank. Even Mayor William Ela, a renowned horseman, rode bicycles.

By the 1880s, the high wheelers – the bikes with the large front wheels that had dominated the 1870s – were being replaced by more modern-style machines, called "safety bikes." They had front and rear wheels about the same size. They had chain-driven rear wheels, powered by pedals under the rider's seat, and they had pneumatic tires. The tires were sometimes filled with buttermilk to prevent flats, and some early riders were known as "Buttermilk Boys." Most of the early "safety bikes" were fixed-gear machines, Brown said. There was no coasting with pedals at rest. When the rear wheel turned, the pedals turned. To stop, one had to halt the pedals. It was not easy to do quickly.

Brown's book tracks the fictional experiences of an unnamed man who, in the 21st century, finds a "mysteriously futuristic and charmingly antiquated" bicycle in the desert near the Lunch Loops bicycle trails west of Grand Junction. The bike turns out to be a chain-and-wheel time machine that takes the man on a journey through the decades of Grand Junction history up to 2015. The book was made into a folk/jazz opera called "One Bike" by the Mesa County Historical Society and performed at Colorado Mesa University in 2021.

Although the main character in "Bicycle Junction" is fictional, he encounters many real people from Grand Junction's history. The book also recounts some of the interesting biking events in the community's past.

For instance, an 1898 race was sponsored by Sam McMullin, who also rode in the race. It was an eight-mile time trial from Main Street, east on D Road toward what was then the Teller Indian School, then back to the starting line. The surprise winner was John L. Gray, a 300-pound lawyer from Montrose, Colorado. But suspicions arose quickly about Gray's victory, even though he was given a 14-minute handicap. Gray was stripped of his win after he admitted he had ridden only to Ninth and Main Streets, then hidden under a bush while the other riders passed, before remounting his bike to arrive at the finish line ahead of everyone else. After Gray was disqualified, a man named Dr. Warner was declared the winner.

"Bicycle Junction" relates other stories, such as a ring of bicycle thieves who stole 25 bikes in Grand Junction in 1901 or the people who passed through the community on long-distance bike rides.

A 23-mile race from Basalt to Glenwood Springs attracted riders from around the state. Grand Junction wheelmen performed well in that contest, winning the race on several occasions. Sponsored by the Colorado Midland Railway, the race began in 1899, and in less than a decade it was attracting hordes of spectators as well as riders. In 1907, the *Sentinel* estimated that more than 500 people from Grand Junction and Palisade rode the special Midland train to Glenwood Springs to watch the end of the race. The same train brought spectators and local race participants back to Grand Junction.

But not everyone took the train. A number of riders from the Fruita Social Wheel Club rode their bikes more than 100 miles each year to watch the end of the race in Glenwood, then took the train home after the race. Their rides

Grand Junction Wheel Club on South Ninth Street – Members of the Grand Junction, Colorado, Wheel Club line up on South Ninth Street in late 19th century. *Courtesy of Chris Brown, Brown Cycles.*

were the inspiration for the L'Eroica Historic 102 Mile Bike Ride from Grand Junction to Glenwood Springs, which Brown organized in 2013. It was held annually for six years.

While male riders garnered most early bicycling headlines, a few women also won renown. Dora Reinhardt, or Rinehart, of Denver became known for long-distance rides. In 1895, she rode 100 miles each day for 20 consecutive days, on a single-speed, steel bike.

Reinhardt's exploits were unusual, but female bicyclists were common by the end of the 19th century. It was not always easy, however.

"It was rare for women to ride initially," Brown said. Their clothing – dresses with multiple petticoats – and Victorian mores that frowned on women showing their ankles discouraged many women from riding.

Moreover, some publications of the time clearly sought to dissuade women from riding. An 1897 brief in the *Aspen Times* illustrates this tendency: "How can bicycle riding be good for girls, when it develops a set of muscles they can't use in cooking?" the newspaper asked. "Girls don't stir cake with their feet."

However, both fashions and attitudes were already changing when that

snarky comment was published. In 1896, women's activist Susan B. Anthony declared of the bicycle that "it has done more to emancipate women than anything else in the world. It gives women a feeling of freedom and self-reliance."

By the 1920s, males and females alike were winning prizes in local bicycle competitions. And bicycles were an important part of Western Colorado's transportation, recreation and social scenes.

Sources: "Bicycle Junction," by Chris Brown; Author interview with Chris Brown; Historic editions of The Daily Sentinel at www.newspapers.com; historic editions of other newspapers at www.coloradohistoricnewspapers.org.

CHAPTER 38:
NATIONAL WILDERNESS CONCEPTS WERE
FORGED AROUND COLORADO LAKE

Arthur Carhart was 27 years old and the first landscape architect to work for the U.S. Forest Service when, on December 10, 1919, he wrote a memorandum to Aldo Leopold, another Forest Service employee who was already beginning to make a name for himself as a conservationist. The subject of the letter was the need to protect *some* federal forest lands from road-building, timbering, cabin-construction and other development.

Inspired by the landscape surrounding Trappers Lake on the White River Forest Reserve in Northwestern Colorado, Carhart wrote: "There is a limit to the number of lands of shore line on the lakes; there is a limit to the number of lakes in existence; there is a limit to the mountainous areas of the world, and in each one of these situations there are portions of natural scenic beauty which are God-made, and the beauties of which ... should be the property of all people."

That memorandum became "one of the most significant records in the history of the wilderness concept," according to the website for the federal government's multi-agency Arthur Carhart National Wilderness Training Center in Missoula, Montana.

Although others also expressed new conservation ideas in the early decades of the 20th century, at the end of World War I, the U.S. Forest Service focused primarily on timbering, grazing, building roads to accommodate those uses and to serve the increasing number of citizens with automobiles eager to visit their public lands.

With this attitude in mind, Carhart was assigned in July 1919 to survey Trappers Lake and develop a plan for laying out several hundred summer home lots around the lake. Carhart worked on the project for several weeks, then returned to his superiors in Denver with a recommendation that the best way to serve the public was to leave the Trappers Lake shoreline unmarred by houses and roads. It was a radical recommendation from a young forest employee. But Carhart was convinced not only of the need to protect Trappers Lake, but of the value to the country of keeping parts of the nation's public lands in their natural state. As a Christian, Carhart believed that if people paid attention to what they encountered in the backcountry, they would "hear the voice of God," said author Tom Wolf, who wrote a biography of Carhart. "He really meant it when

Carhart canoe – Wilderness advocate Arthur Carhart, after he left Colorado and was working at what would later become the Boundary Waters Canoe Area Wilderness in the Superior National Forest in Minnesota. *Public Domain, U.S. Forest Service.*

he said that public lands recreation would make people better Americans."

Leopold learned of Carhart's recommendation during a Forest Service meeting in Salt Lake City in November 1919. Intrigued, Leopold, then 33, met Carhart in Denver on December 6, 1919. He asked the younger man to explain in writing his thoughts on preserving wild lands. The result was the "Memorandum for Mr. Leopold, District 3," quoted above.

The Forest Service acted on Carhart's recommendation by administratively protecting Trappers Lake in 1920. A road was built to the edge of the lake, and a lodge was allowed there. A cabin for Forest Service use near the shores of Trappers Lake was left standing, but no other roads or structures have been built. Today the lake is part of the Flat Tops Wilderness in the White River National Forest.

Aldo Leopold, then an assistant district forester in New Mexico, had been contemplating ways of protecting parts of the Gila National Forest in western New Mexico. With his urging, the Gila Wilderness Area became the first administratively designated wilderness area in 1924. But it would be another 40 years before Congress adopted the 1964 Wilderness Act and began to legislatively designate certain natural areas as wilderness.

For much of this nation's history, wilderness was viewed as something to be tamed or conquered. It was an impediment to civilization, agriculture and industry. But in the 19th century, a few voices had begun to speak out on the need to protect parts of the natural world.

- In the 1820s, author James Fennimore Cooper began to achieve fame with the first of his Leatherstocking novels. Characters in his early novels declared the importance of preserving and protecting the natural world.

- In the 1830s, artist George Catlin, known for his paintings of Native Americans, offered one of the earliest ideas for a national park, which, he suggested should include not only wild lands and creatures, but Native people: "A nation's Park, containing man and beast in all the wild and freshness of their nature's beauty," he explained in a letter to a friend.

- Henry David Thoreau proclaimed in 1862, "In Wilderness is the preservation of the World."

- In 1872, the United States established the first national park in the world. The legislation that created Yellowstone National Park mandated regulations to preserve the park's natural resources "in their natural condition."

- The nation also began working to protect its once-vast forest resources while still allowing uses such as logging, grazing, and recreation. This culminated with creation of the U.S. Forest Service within the Department of Agriculture in 1905.

• At the end of the 19th century, a growing number of people, John Muir prominent among them, argued for more national parks and protection of more wild lands.

• In 1935, a handful of people including Leopold and Bob Marshall formed The Wilderness Society and encouraged Congress to adopt wilderness legislation. But it took many years of negotiating and numerous drafts of the legislation before Congress finally adopted the 1964 Wilderness Act.

One of the major congressional obstacles was Colorado Congressman Wayne Aspinall, who lived in Palisade, Colorado. He blocked multiple attempts to pass a wilderness bill. He finally allowed the bill to proceed in 1963, when he won concessions from conservationists to protect Colorado's ability to develop and use its water, and to make sure ranchers could adequately maintain their grazing permits in wilderness. The next year, the Wilderness Act was passed, protecting public lands that were supposed to be "untrammeled by man, where man himself is a visitor who does not remain."

The Act set aside 9.1 million acres in 54 wilderness areas. The Flat Tops Wilderness Area, including Trappers Lake, and the Gila Wilderness Area were included in the 1964 act. Interestingly, Arthur Carhart didn't support the final bill because he thought too many compromises had been made.

The 1964 legislation also authorized Congress – and only Congress – to consider more lands for wilderness designation. In the subsequent decades, multiple bills have passed to designate new wilderness areas and expand existing ones. As of 2022, there were 111 million acres of designated wilderness in the United States, with a substantial amount of that in Alaska. The wilderness areas are managed for the public primarily by the Forest Service, the Bureau of Land Management, the National Park Service and the U.S. Fish and Wildlife Service.

But it took the efforts of two determined young foresters in 1919 to get the ball rolling.

Arthur Carhart left the White River National Forest soon after his memorandum to Leopold. He worked in recreation planning and designed campgrounds in the San Isabell National Forest near Pueblo, Colorado. Then he moved east and led the effort to protect what became the Forest Service's Boundary Waters Canoe Area Wilderness in northern Minnesota. He returned to Colorado in the 1930s and wrote several books about this state, its history and natural resources. He died in 1978 in California.

Aldo Leopold remained with the Forest Service in New Mexico until 1924, then moved his large family to Wisconsin, where he held several jobs before he joined the faculty of the University of Wisconsin. He became the first collegiate professor of game management in the United States. He also became an outspo-ken advocate for conservation and hunting, through his writing, by joining the Wilderness Society and other organizations. He acquired a small farm along the Wisconsin River in central Wisconsin, where he wrote his famous book, *A Sand County Almanac*. He died while fighting a grass fire at the farm in 1948.

The ideas he and Carhart discussed more than a century ago, beginning with Trappers Lake in northwestern Colorado, were instrumental in forging the system of wilderness lands so many people enjoy today.

Sources: The Arthur Carhart National Wilderness Training Center in Missoula, Mont., www.carhart.wilderness.net/;"Aldo Leopold;" by Curtis Meine; "Arthur Carhart: Wilderness Prophet," by Tom Wolf; "Water, Wilderness and Wayne Aspinall," by Steven C. Shulte; "How National Forest Recreation Planning Got Its Start in Southern Colorado 100 Years Ago," by Shanna Lewis, Colorado Public Radio, June 23, 2020, www.cpr.org; online information about the White River and Gila National Forests at www.fs.usda.gov.

CHAPTER 39:
HANGING LAKE HAS LONG ATTRACTED TRAVELERS AND TOURISTS

In the first years of the 20th century, the Taylor State Road connected Denver and Grand Junction, Colorado, carving its way through Glenwood Canyon near Glenwood Springs, Colorado. Almost immediately after the single-lane dirt road was established on the north side of the river, people discovered a scenic wonder called Hanging Lake. More than 120 years later, it remains one of the most visited tourist attractions in Western Colorado.

In 1902, an article in a Fort Collins newspaper described the lake as "one of the most beautiful lakes the mind can conceive of." A 1903 article in the *Glenwood Avalanche* called Hanging Lake and the falls above it the "Yosemite of Garfield." It recounted a first-hand account of a hike up the 1.5-mile trail. "It may be shorter, but because of the steady climb, it would be better to put it at two miles. It took this party two hours, including three short rests, to get to the lake."

By 1908, one could purchase postcards with a colorized photo of Hanging Lake. And, during the teens, auto trips, hikes, and picnics at Hanging Lake occurred regularly. It was in the 1920s, however, when Hanging Lake tourism really exploded. Throughout that decade, *The Daily Sentinel* in Grand Junction, Colorado, carried frequent notices such as this one from August 1923: "H.G. DeWalt, wife and sister ... just returned from a week's trip to Glenwood Springs, made several trips, one was to Hanging Lake, which was of much interest to all." Youth groups and professional organizations also made regular trips to what one 1927 *Sentinel* article incorrectly declared was "the only hanging lake in the world."

A few similar lakes exist around the world. But "Hanging Lake is unique in the [Southern Rockies] as a lake formed by travertine deposition," according to a 2010 evaluation of the lake for designation as a National Natural Landmark. Travertine lakes are created by calcium carbonate deposits. In contrast, most natural lakes in the southern Rocky Mountains were formed by glaciers.

Native Americans had been to the shores of Hanging Lake long before Europeans arrived, but the first white man known to have visited the lake did not arrive until the late 19th century, when he was prospecting for gold along the Colorado River, then known as the Grand. The unnamed prospector supposedly found a horse carcass at the mouth of a creek that flowed into the river and

therefore named it Dead Horse Creek. He prospected up the creek and found Hanging Lake, but little gold.

About the turn of the 20th century, Thomas Bailey and Clarence Wayne homesteaded the land from the mouth of Dead Horse Creek to Hanging Lake. However, they apparently never obtained title to the land. In 1912, for $953, the city of Glenwood Springs purchased 760 acres of federal land that included the Hanging Lake Trail and the lake itself.

By the 1930s, Hanging Lake Park, as it was called, was developing a reputation beyond Western Colorado, as it was often mentioned in newspapers around the state. Meanwhile, advertisements in the *Sentinel* asked: "Why Not Hanging Lake Park for Sunday Dinner?" A restaurant at the park offered beef and pork dinners for 45 cents each. Fried chicken dinners were 75 cents.

Also in the 1930s, the Civilian Conservation Corps, created to help provide jobs during the Great Depression, began improving the Hanging Lake Trail. "The trail to the lake is being widened and new bridges are being constructed," the *Sentinel* reported in July 1936. Three years later, the paper noted that CCC crews were going to construct a wooden shelter halfway up the trail.

In 1938, another notice in the *Sentinel* mentioned a service station at the base of the Hanging Lake trail, operated by Roy Pratt. However, in 1943, the *Sentinel* reported that Pratt and his wife had sold their Hanging Lake property to W.S. Speer of Palisade, Colorado. The sale "included the Hanging Lake Service station, cottages, café and equipment," the paper said.

By 1945, the couple associated with the resort for the longest time – G.O. "Dub" Danforth and his wife – had acquired the resort. Two years later, they apparently decided to lease the property. In October of that year, the *Sentinel* announced that John D. Dawson and his wife, formerly of Grand Junction, "are now operating Hanging Lake Inn, 10 miles from Glenwood Springs." But the Dawsons were not associated with the resort for long, because by the early 1950s, the Danforths were back in charge.

The 1950s were a busy time for Hanging Lake and the resort. Tourists could rent horses that would take them three-quarters of the way to the lake. But they would have to tie the animals and hike the steepest part of the trail. Western artist Jack Roberts took up residence in a cabin at Hanging Lake. Newspaper articles about him and his paintings of cowboys, Native Americans and West-

---

Photo on previous page: 1917 picnic – Visitors enjoy Hanging Lake, above Glenwood Canyon, near Glenwood Springs, Colorado, circa 1917. *Image courtesy of the Eagle County Historical Society, Eagle Valley Library District.*

ern landscapes brought more attention to the lake and resort.

Then there were boat races. For a half-dozen years, a Grand Junction-based group called Colorado River Skippers sponsored motorboat races on the reservoir that was created on the river by Shoshone Dam, whose primary purpose was to create hydroelectric power. The power plant is still in operation in the 21st century. The races were part of Glenwood Springs' Strawberry Days celebration, and in some years, water skiing demonstrations were held between races. Danforth was involved, as well, helping to move a boat dock to the lake for the races. It's not clear from newspaper articles why the races ended, but parking along what was then a two-lane highway was always a problem. When a toddler was injured by a car while trying to cross the highway during the boat races, it may have been marked the end for the races.

The 1950s also offered a foreshadowing of more recent events in Glenwood Canyon. On July 17, 1954, a large mudslide carried rocks and boulders down Dead Horse Creek, closing what was then U.S. Highway 6&24 for more than 24 hours.

Big changes occurred in the 1960s. In March 1968, the resort was closed and all of its equipment, furniture, tools and other items were sold at auction. By then it was clear the city of Glenwood Springs was going to abandon its ownership of Hanging Lake. In May 1969, after 45 years of city control, the Glenwood Springs City Council finalized its decision to turn the property over to the White River National Forest. That did not change the popularity of Hanging Lake, however. At the end of 1972, the Forest Service reported that 16,000 hikers had trekked up the Hanging Lake Trail that year.

But more changes were coming in the 1970s. Planning was underway for the construction of four-lane Interstate 70 through the canyon. And, with even more visitors anticipated, the 1.5-mile trail to the lake was slated for its first major improvements since the Civilian Conservation Corps years. Jerry Craghead, who served as trail crew foreman for the work, recalled that members of the crew, which included women, each hiked the trail several times a day carrying 90-pound packs of concrete on World War II-era pack boards. When vandals destroyed some of the work that had just been completed, crew members were devastated. But they continued on, this time with the help of horses and mules, to complete the project.

In the 21st century, trail improvements were conducted in 2010 and again in 2015. And the number of annual visitors exploded to 186,000 by 2018, forcing the Forest Service to institute a permit system for those hiking to the lake. But a major forest fire in 2020, followed by mudslides in 2021, closed the trail again. It was re-opened in 2022, after the completion of preliminary trail improvements. Meanwhile, White River National Forest personnel were designing more permanent trail improvements and a realignment project to keep one of the most popular tourist attractions in Colorado open and accessible to visitors willing to make the strenuous hike.

Sources: Historic newspapers at www.newspapers.com and www.coloradohistoricnewspapers.org; Hanging Lake information compiled by Bill Johnson and by the White River National Forest; "Evaluation of Hanging Lake for its Merit in Meeting National Significance Criteria as a National Natural Landmark," by Karin Decker; Author interviews with Jerry Craghead, Bill Johnson and White River National Forest spokesman David Boyd.

CHAPTER 40:
RECREATIONAL SKIING HAS A LONG
HISTORY IN WESTERN COLORADO

In January 1931, four Grand Junction, Colorado, men traveled to Mesa Lakes Resort on Grand Mesa and, over four days, they built the first ski run on the mountain. "While there, they made a ski run about one half mile in length," *The Daily Sentinel* in Grand Junction reported on February 3, 1931. The run was likely adjacent to Mesa Lakes Resort, a small private business that rented cabins and mostly served summer visitors.

Because winter sports in the 1930s often involved ski jumping, the *Sentinel* said the men also built a small jump. The four men – Russel Sisac, Richard Manning, Harry Peck and Roger Nash – hoped to promote winter sports and possibly create a permanent ski resort at Mesa Lakes, along with ice skating rinks and a toboggan course.

There was plenty of precedent for them to imitate in Colorado. Howelsen Hill near Steamboat Springs was founded in 1914 by Norwegian immigrant Carl Howelsen. It was still in business in the early 21st century and was known as the oldest operating ski area in North America. Additionally, by the 1930s dozens of small ski areas operated in the state, mostly using rope tows. Some places, such as Aspen, used a boat tow – a rough wooden toboggan that could seat a half-dozen people and was pulled slowly up the mountain by rope. The first chairlift was built north of Gunnison using old mining tram cables and hand-constructed chairs.

Within a few years, other ski runs opened on Grand Mesa, but most only operated briefly. One was established part-way up Land's End Road in 1935. It had a single, narrow run, in some places only eight feet wide. Also, "No tow of any kind ever existed at this site," wrote Steve Lambert, in his history of skiing on Grand Mesa. "Uphill travel was accomplished by means of a herringbone climb." Because of its southwestern exposure, it only lasted two seasons.

Another ski run was built near Cedaredge, Colorado, and one near where Vega Reservoir now sits. But it was the area adjacent to Mesa Lakes Resort that attracted the most visitors and proved the most resilient. The Grand Junction Ski Club continued to operate the area for minimal fees, and by 1937, the club had 150 members. A rope tow, powered by a Ford Model T engine, propelled skiers up the quarter-mile run. U.S. Secretary of Interior Harold Ickes reportedly visited the Mesa Lakes ski run during the 1938-39 season.

Cooper Hill – Skiing on Cooper Hill, near Camp Hale and Leadville, Colorado, circa late 1940s. *Image courtesy of the Eagle County Historical Society, Eagle Valley Library District.*

By 1941, however, the ski club was looking for a location with more territory for skiing and better access for skiers. Club leaders settled on Mesa Creek Ski Area, with its base where an old wagon crossed Mesa Creek, several miles below Mesa Lakes Resort. Another automobile-powered rope tow was installed, and an old building from the Depression-era Civilian Conservation Corps was used as the ski lodge. Ski traffic grew each year, except for a couple of years during World War II, and by 1960, club leaders were again looking for another location. After a successful community fund-raising drive, in December 1966, the Powderhorn Ski Area, now called Powderhorn Mountain Resort, opened to the public. It has continued to operate ever since under a variety of management organizations.

Recreational skiing in Colorado did not begin with small ski areas and rope tows. It was a natural outgrowth of skis used for winter transportation. Scandinavian immigrants brought the long wooden planks with upturned ends to Colorado and the rest of North America. Although they were cumbersome, many people found the devices, which were initially called Norwegian snowshoes, better for getting around in deep snow than traditional Native American snowshoes. In Colorado, miners used them to travel to and from their mines when snow was deep. Ministers, mail carriers and midwives all used skis to get around in the high country. During the late 1860s, Methodist minister and postman John Dyer made a week-long ski circuit from Fairplay to Alma, then over Mosquito Pass to Oro City, where Leadville, Colorado, would later boom.

In addition to using skis for transportation, many early Coloradans also viewed skiing as a form of sport. The first downhill ski contests in the United States may have been held in Crested Butte and Gunnison, Colorado, in 1886. A racing club was formed by local miners at Irwin, near Crested Butte, as early as 1883. These skiers used simple straps on 10-foot-long skis and a single pole to guide and help them brake. They took their lives in their hands when they descended steep slopes.

In the early 1900s, Howelsen and others began to get airborne on wooden slats, and ski jumping became an international sport. There were competitions in Europe, Canada, the eastern United States, Wisconsin, and Michigan, Colorado, and much of the Rocky Mountain West. It became an Olympic event in 1924. In the 1930s, *The Daily Sentinel* reported regularly on these events in Colorado and around the country. It also reported accidents and fatalities in the sport.

Additionally, during the 1930s, stores in Grand Junction advertised skis for sale among their winter goods. And skis were still used for winter transportation as well as sport. The Sentinel reported on people using skis to check on irrigation reservoirs on Grand Mesa.

Although the 1930s saw the beginnings of many ski areas in Colorado, it wasn't until World War II and the following decades that ski resorts and recreational skiing really boomed. Much of that began with Camp Hale, near Leadville, Colorado. It was the training ground for the U.S. Army's 10th Mountain Division, which distinguished itself in mountain combat in Italy during the war. In 2022, the site was designated as Camp Hale-Continental Divide National Monument by President Joe Biden.

To instruct the 10th Mountain soldiers in downhill skiing, the Army built a ski run at the top of Tennessee Pass, with what was then the longest T-bar lift in the world. This was Cooper Hill, which was eventually turned over to civilians and still operates today.

Some 10,000 men trained at Camp Hale during its years as a military camp. A number of them helped shape Colorado's ski industry in the post-war years. Men such as Friedl Pfeifer and Fritz Benedict were instrumental in developing Aspen and surrounding ski areas. Peter Seibert and Robert Parker initially went to Aspen after the war, but later teamed up with others to found a ski resort and town at Vail, Colorado. Other 10th Mountain alumni went to Steamboat Springs, Winter Park, and Breckenridge or participated in creating Colorado Ski Country USA. Gordy Wren worked at Steamboat Springs and other resorts. He also conducted one of the surveys that led to the U.S. Forest Service to approve development of Powderhorn Ski Area on Grand Mesa.

Meanwhile, other small ski areas were being established around the state – near Glenwood Springs, on Monarch, Wolf Creek, and Loveland passes and near Durango. The city of Denver spent significant amounts of money to develop Winter Park and to encourage people to ride a ski train to the resort.

In Aspen, however, Walter and Elizabeth Paepcke had a much grander idea. They envisioned an international resort that would attract not only winter sports enthusiasts, but intellectuals and music lovers to the one-time mining community. Working with Pfeifer, Benedict and mining heir Darcy Brown, the Paepckes redesigned the Aspen ski area on a much larger scale. Chairlifts were installed and new runs constructed. The revamped mountain opened in January of 1947. Not long afterward, the Paepckes established the Aspen Institute for Humanistic Studies, now known simply as the Aspen Institute.

Soon, other ski areas began seeking broader visitor bases. Steamboat Springs, with its long history of skiing, was among the first. Then Vail was established, opening in December of 1962. Crested Butte, Breckenridge, Telluride, Copper Mountain, and Keystone sought to attract skiers from around the country and the world. Smaller areas such as Powderhorn, Sunlight, Purgatory, Loveland and Cooper Hill also attracted outside visitors while continuing to cater to local skiers.

Many other small areas were created but failed. Meanwhile, snowboarding took off and cross-country skiing continued to grow.

Another change has been the development back-country ski trekking to untrammeled mountain slopes, from where the trekkers can make downhill runs without encountering hordes of skiers who rode ski lifts to groomed ski runs. These 21st century back-country skiers, who attach "skins" made of nylon, mohair, rubber, and carbon filaments to "skin up" mountain slopes so they can ski down them, didn't invent the technique, however. In the 1930s, Grand Junction Ski Club members attempting to reach their ski area near Mesa Lakes Resort often found the road blocked by heavy snowfall. Frequently they conducted all-day, uphill ski treks from the town of Mesa to the resort, Lambert wrote. "Socks" or "skins" made of either burlap or canvas were strapped to the bottom of their skis to assist them in climbing up the mountain.

Evolving ski technology, like skiing itself, has a long history among the multitudes of outdoor enthusiasts in Colorado.

Sources: "From Trail to Throngs – A History of Mesa Creek and Powderhorn Ski Areas," academic paper by Steve Lambert; historic editions of The Daily Sentinel at www.newspapers.com; "A History of Skiing in Colorado," by Abbott Fay; "Some Local Skiing History," www.mesacountylibraries.org; "The Interesting History of Colorado Ski Country," by Justin Cygan, www.coloradoski.com.

INDEX

ACKNOWLEDGEMENTS

———

So many people have provided information and suggestions to me for the history columns that became the chapters in this book that it would be impossible for me to name all of them. Suffice it to say I thank all these people and all the readers of my "First Draft" columns in *The Daily Sentinel*. They continue to make "First Draft" a popular feature at gjsentinel.com. They have made it a pleasure for me to keep writing the columns and to collect them in this book.

Beyond those folks, I want to specifically thank those people whose help made this book possible:

First, there is my wife Judy, who proofread each of these columns before they appeared in the Sentinel, correcting spelling and grammar errors and pointing out holes in the narratives. Additionally, she has joined me on many trips to conduct historical research and has quietly supported me as I hid out in my home office to prepare this book.

Next, is Sherida Warner, a colleague from the days when I worked full time at the *Sentinel* and a wonderful editor. She agreed to edit the manuscript for this book and has done a masterful job.

I am grateful to Danny Rosen and his staff at the Lithic Press and Lithic Bookstore in Fruita, Colorado, for agreeing to publish this book and for allowing me to work with them on the layout of the book to make sure we can all be proud of it.

Once more, my appreciation to Jay Seaton, publisher of *The Daily Sentinel*, for allowing me to use the columns originally published in the *Sentinel* as chapters in this book. And thanks to all the staff at the *Sentinel* over the years who had a hand in editing my First Draft columns. Most recently, they included Editor Dale Shrull, City Editor Tom Hess and Sherida Warner.

I am indebted to several people and organizations for helping me find photographs and obtain permission for the photos that appear in this book. They include:

- Matti Fisher at the Museums of Western Colorado in Grand Junction.
- Priscilla Walker with the Palisade Historical Society in Palisade.
- The Ela Family – Shirley, Steve and Tom Ela – in Hotchkiss and in Grand Junction.

- Dan Davidson with the Museum of Northwest Colorado in Craig.
- Kathy Heicher with the Eagle County Historical Society in Eagle.
- Matthew Mickelson with Eagle Valley Library District.
- James K. Wetzel of the Delta County Historical Society in Delta.
- Jane Thompson with Rimrocker Historical Society in Nucla.
- Michelle Fuller of the Uintah County Library Regional History Center, Vernal, Utah.
- History Colorado.

More than anything, my sincere appreciation to all of you who think the stories I write are worth reading.

Robert Silbernagel has been writing about history in newspapers, magazines and books since 1975. He retired as the editorial page editor of The Daily Sentinel in Grand Junction, Colorado, and currently writes a history column for the newspaper. He is an avid horseman and enjoys outdoor activities in the West, as well as reading and writing about history.